Sissinghurst

Portrait of a Garden

❧ Published in Association with The National Trust

Sissinghurst

Portrait of a Garden

Jane Brown
Photographs by John Miller

PHOENIX ILLUSTRATED

First published in 1994 by
George Weidenfeld & Nicolson Ltd

This paperback edition first published in 1998 by
Phoenix Illustrated
Orion Publishing Group,
Orion House,
5, Upper St. Martin's Lane
London WC2H 9EA

British Library Cataloguing-in-Publication Data
A catalogue record for this book is available from the British Library

ISBN 0753804379

Designed by Rita Wüthrich
Phototypeset by Keyspools, Globorne, Lancs
Colour separations by Newsele Litho Limited
Printed in Italy by Printers Srl, Trento

Half-title page: An aerial view of Sissinghurst
Title-page: Sissinghurst Crescent; the seat is one of three in the garden designed by Edwin Lutyens

Acknowledgements

John Miller and I would like to record our thanks to Nigel Nicolson, and to Arland Kingston, Paul Wood, Pamela Schwerdt and Sibylle Kreutzberger, for allowing us to produce this book. My further thanks go to Miss Schwerdt and Miss Kreutzberger and their colleagues of the National Trust, past and present, who have advised upon my manuscript. I am grateful to John and Rosemary Beale and Pamela Kilbane who, as they did with my previous book, *Vita's Other World*, have encouraged and added to my understanding of Sissinghurst. I am also grateful to the Estate of Richard Church for permission to use my final quotation.

Jane Brown

Photographic Acknowledgements

The publishers would like to thank the following people for their kind permission to reproduce the black-and-white illustrations on the pages listed below:
Edwin Smith 32 and 74; Harry Smith Collection 126; Aerofilms Ltd 26; Lord Sackville 9; Nigel Nicolson 12 and 25.

The black-and-white photograph on page 38 was taken by John Miller and the colour photograph on the half-title page by Patrick Sutherland. They are both copyright of Weidenfeld and Nicolson. The map on page 131 was drawn by Christine and Stuart Page and is copyright of the National Trust.

Editorial Note

The colour photographs for this book were taken throughout 1988 and 1989. Where relevant, the month is given in the captions but please note that the winter of 1988–9 was exceptionally mild and that the summer of 1989 was exceptionally hot and dry.

CONTENTS

FOREWORD

The great gale of October 1987 and its gentler daughter of January 1990 (gentler, that is, for Kent) have created at Sissinghurst an unexpected benefit, by opening a vista of the Castle from the main road. The roseate brick tower is suddenly seen at half-a-mile's distance across the orchards and startles many a casual motorist into turning aside for a closer look. What they will find are the quite substantial relics of an Elizabethan manor, now more like a village in appearance than a house because its surviving buildings lie apart from one another, and spread among them a garden which has become one of the most famous in England, and hence by definition in the world.

It is the creation of two people, Vita Sackville-West and her husband Harold Nicolson, who bought the property in 1930 as a near-ruin set in a wasteland, and steadily worked on it and in it until Vita died there in 1962. Harold lived another six years, long enough to see it pass into the ownership of the National Trust.

People who like to boast of their long and deep acquaintance with the place are apt to say that Sissinghurst is no longer what it was 'in Vita's day', implying that it has lost something of its serenity and betrayed her genius. Let the reply be this: that no garden is, or should ever be, what it was, since it is a living, growing, changing thing, and it would be foolish, unimaginative and actually treacherous to Vita's own conception of a garden, to replace every plant that dies and every tree that topples over by the same plant or same tree. This of course applies provided that nothing is done that conflicts with the architecture of the place (a shrub that interrupts a vista) or its colour-scheme (rhododendrons in place of their tenderer cousin, the azalea), and that everything new should be in spirit faithful to the date of the garden's origins, the mid-twentieth century, for Sissinghurst is in one sense an historical document. If Vita could revisit it today, she might exclaim, 'Oh not gentians *there*!', and not know quite what to think about the 166,000 visitors, their car park, shop, restaurant and loos, but she would be happily astounded that her garden has survived her by thirty years without any essential change within the encircling moat and walls.

But change there has been and will be, and that makes it all the more important to record how they started the garden, with what ideas and influences they began (Harold planning, Vita planting), and how rapidly their projects became reality. This is what Jane Brown has done. In her earlier book *Vita's Other World* (Viking, 1985) she explored Vita's gardening experience at Knole, Constantinople and Long Barn. Here she focuses upon its consummation, Sissinghurst, beginning with a brief historical account of the place, tracing its transformation by the Nicolsons in the 1930s and its survival during the War, and ending with what is the main purpose of her book, to consider the artistry of each individual garden and the unity of the whole.

She has accomplished her self-set task with enviable perspicacity and skill. I, who saw Sissinghurst emerge from cabbage stalks and discarded tins and bottles and still walk its paths every day, should know it better than Jane Brown who can be only an occasional visitor and never knew my mother. But it is not so. She reveals to me much that I have often seen but never noticed, like the juxtaposition of a group of flowers or the siting of a statue, and attributes to different parts of the garden human characteristics that show her intimacy with them, like the 'cheerfulness' of the cottage garden or the 'phenomenal child' of the White. She gives every visitor, and indeed every resident, a new perspective on a garden of perspectives. I wish that I could write such a book about a place I love and I am grateful to Jane Brown for having written it.

Nigel Nicolson

Sissinghurst, February 1990

FOLLOWING IN QUEEN ELIZABETH'S FOOTSTEPS

On 26 August 1899, to mark a royal visit to the Sackvilles' magnificent Knole in Kent, reputedly the largest private house in England, the inevitable group photograph was taken. This faded image above shows seven solemn gentlemen, four grand ladies and one small girl, who wait around the tea table while the photographer from Sevenoaks, Mr Essenhighe Corke, takes his time. Lady Sackville presides, looking more imperious than any queen, and the shy Duchess of York, the future Queen Mary, sits on her left. At the Duchess's feet is an angelic looking seven-year old, who smiles from beneath her enormous hat piled with flowers. This is Victoria Mary Sackville-West, known as Vita; she sits on the grass at Knole as the heiress to thirteen generations of Sackvilles who had loved that great house. Queen Elizabeth I gave Knole to her Lord High Treasurer,

Above *The royal tea-party at Knole in August 1899.*
Left *Sissinghurst Castle, the west entrance front. (October)*

Right *The orchard from the tower; four hundred years ago this view would have revealed the* cour d'honneur *of the Bakers' house. The South Cottage, on the right, is all that remains of the Tudor court, and was the cornerpiece of the south and east ranges. The east range of buildings crossed the orchard to where the north range completed the court, in line with the present Bishopsgate wall. The court itself was gravelled and had a paved edging, and the surrounding buildings were composed of two storeys of patterned brick, with a third storey of attics and gable rooms. The moat wall, seen on the far right, is possibly a relic of the medieval manor house, which stood farther out in the orchard, closer to the moat. (May)*

Above *The entrance arch, looking through the tower and beyond to the orchard. This vista is essentially the one which awaited Queen Elizabeth I's arrival at Sissinghurst in 1573. The tower was newly built by her host Richard Baker, though it then had steps, where he and his wife Catherine stood with a welcoming present of a silver cup. The legend of Sissinghurst is that the Queen's footsteps could not be raked away from the soil, and when paving was laid her imprints still glittered in the dark. This paving was laid in the 1930s and needed to be relaid by the National Trust in the late 1960s. (November)*

Above *Sissinghurst from the north-east, looking across the present orchard from where the gazebo now stands, as it was drawn by F. Grose in 1760, when the house was being used to incarcerate French prisoners-of-war. This drawing clearly shows the Priest's House, standing a little apart on the right, and the jumbled and haphazard nature of the servants' quarters at the rear of the cour d'honneur, which were obviously built of timber and lathe, as they are at Knole.*

Below *Medieval brickwork survives in the gables of the entrance front.*

Thomas Sackville, and it passed down those succeeding generations by virtue of Thomas's fruitful and wise marriage to Cecilie Baker of Sissinghurst.

The enchantment that Sissinghurst Castle exerts today is largely the gift of Cecilie Baker's heirs and successors. Here the Bakers, their lords, ladies and monarchs, the shadows of Manns and Cornwallises, of Edward Gibbon and the wretched French prisoners he guarded, of Vita Sackville-West and Harold Nicolson and their friends, and today's guardians, all present themselves as part of the cavalcade that serves the spirit of this place.

'... it may, I think, fairly be claimed that the spirit of the place is very strong at Sissinghurst ...' wrote Vita Sackville-West in 1942. 'This is proved by the fact that visitors nearly always say one of two things about it, sometimes both. One waits for the remark and is seldom disappointed. The better-informed visitor says that it reminds him of manor houses in Normandy. The more instinctive visitor exclaims that it is like the castle of Sleeping Beauty. There is truth in both ...'[1]

Sissinghurst finds its name and a misty pedigree with a first mention, in 1180, as the home of a Stephen de Saxingherste. These de Saxenhursts, or Saxinhersts, and another Norman family, the de Berhams, were the owners of a manor house here for three hundred quiet years, until it was abandoned, perhaps for greener pastures, by Henry de Berham in about 1490.[2] He sold Sissinghurst to an upstart from nearby Cranbrook, named Thomas Baker. What Thomas Baker did with this medieval house is not known; he died in 1497 and his estate passed to his son Richard, who enjoyed it but for a little time before his own death seven years afterwards. In 1504, therefore, Sissinghurst fell to the lot of a young man in his late teens, John Baker, Richard's eldest son, who was in the process of being 'bred to the law'.[3] This medieval house was most likely to have been a timbered building within a moat, and was probably sited on the present orchard. There is also a theory that part of it was brick, for this is good brick-making country, and the range on the right of the present entrance arch, and possibly the moat wall, were part of this earliest house.[4]

The first Baker of sturdiness and substance is young John, who comes into the limelight and brings his house with him. Having become a lawyer he climbed steadily; he became a Bencher of the Inner Temple in 1517, then a Justice of the Peace and Member of Parliament in quick succession. In 1524 he married Catherine Sackville of Buckhurst in Sussex, the daughter of another fast-rising family, but she died the same year, probably in childbirth, and he soon after married a lady called Elizabeth Barrett. By 1536 John Baker

was Attorney General, and earning Henry VIII's favour, he climbed ever higher. He was appointed Henry's Chancellor of the Exchequer in 1540, and then Chancellor of the Court of First Fruits and Tenths, one of those curious political sinecures which yield untold riches to a clever incumbent. Sir John, as he now was, profited well from the Dissolution of the Monasteries, gaining Sussex estates from the New Priory at Hastings and local property which was forfeited by a little chapel, the Trinity Chapel at Milkhouse Street (which is now renamed Sissinghurst village). He has been darkly painted for his time-serving, but his ability to survive was necessary in that treacherous Tudor world; he had been born in Catholic England, and on suddenly finding her to be Protestant had refined the delicate skill of knowing what it was politic to believe. When his patron King Henry VIII died he served the boy King Edward VI, and then – after this royal fifteen-year-old's death, with the rest of the Privy Council – he supported the cause of Lady Jane Grey. But in the nick of time, persuaded by Lords Arundel and Paget in a famous Privy Council meeting, he changed sides and gave the throne to Mary Tudor. Sir John's Catholic loyalties came to the fore again and he served Queen Mary as Chancellor of the Exchequer; the Queen paid him the honour of visiting his country home at Sissinghurst in the summer of 1557. Surely it was his proudest moment, as he accompanied the Queen beneath the entrance arch, but what did he show her? He seems to have been too busy to

Above *Looking north from the tower lawn; a fragment of the wall on the left of the gateway remained from the north range of the old house; the rest of the wall was in ruins and rebuilt by the Nicolsons in the 1930s, when the gateway to the present White Garden was added. The plaque of the three bishops was brought home from Constantinople in 1914 and subsequently moved from the Nicolsons' previous home, Long Barn near Sevenoaks. The Priest's House was either adapted or built in the mid-seventeenth century as a home for Sir Henry Baker's private chaplain; Sir Henry was granted a licence for both chaplain and chapel in 1639 when he complained that the roads to Cranbrook were too difficult and impassable for his family to make regular appearances at church. (May)*

spend much time at Sissinghurst, and yet he must have wanted to build, as did his fellow courtiers, in the fashion set by King Henry VIII. Lord Marney's Layer Marney in Essex and Sir Richard Weston's Sutton Place in Surrey, as well as his Sackville brother-in-law's Bolebroke in Sussex, were all patterns which he would have wanted to emulate. These Tudor lords of building, raisers of gatehouse towers and soaring octagonal towers of brick with stone mullions, barleysugar chimneys and patterns of chevrons and diapers, were Sir John's peers and companions. But it seems that he was too busy to devote as much time to building as he might have liked, and he showed Queen Mary his comfortable, but old, timber house, and perhaps the ideas of what he wanted to build when time allowed.

The year after her visit to Sissinghurst Queen Mary died; Catholic England died with her and Sir John, one of her favourites, was left in a difficult situation. However, he had benefited throughout his career from a canny sense of judgement, and he judged it right to the last, dying in peace just a few weeks after Queen Elizabeth I came to the throne. His son Richard, already established as a quiet and respectable Protestant lawyer, inherited Sissinghurst as his country estate.

Richard was to have all the advantages and none of the risks of his father's position and fortune. He had plenty of time for building, he kept his father's entrance range, and raised his tall slim vantage tower to gaze out over his fields and woods. From the top of Sir Richard's tower today it is possible to imagine the appearance of his house. The entrance court must have been much as we see it, except that it was busy with horses and stable boys; in the opposite direction there was a gravelled *cour d'honneur*, or inner court, which covered the area of the present tower lawn, and extended into the orchard. This court, with a paved rim and a path across its centre, was thought 'perfect and very beautiful' by Horace Walpole writing in the eighteenth century.[5] It was defined on three sides by long ranges of brick and patterned façades, with stone mullions, pedimented doorcases and a little forest of peaked gables and twisted chimneys. On the right, the present South Cottage, was the farthest corner of these buildings, and so the vague markings and the openings in the rose garden wall are the vestiges of the windows and doors of the old south range of galleries and rooms. On the left side of the *cour d'honneur* were the galleries and rooms of the north range, which extended out into the orchard, where the linking range of building stretched southwards, to the South Cottage. Within one of these ranges of buildings was the grandest room, Sissinghurst's long gallery, a 'fine gallery, a hundred and twenty feet by eighteen', taking up the whole of one side of the court, which had a vaulted ceiling and panelling painted in a 'light genteel grotesque'.[6] These are interesting points; eighteen feet is the width Harold Nicolson found when they measured up the entrance range for possible conversion in 1930, so it must have been a standard building width at Sissinghurst. Secondly, the *genteel grotesque* must have sparked a sympathy in Vita's mind, for its nearest counterpart must be in the light grey grisaille of the staircase at Knole, and the Colonnade Room walls of later date, both more than mere decorative effects in her memory.

But to return to Walpole's words, for they are all that there are to describe the Bakers' house (though he was seeing it one hundred and fifty years after Sir Richard Baker's death), he cannot resist a jibe, – 'The whole is built for show, for the back of the house is nothing but lathe and plaster'.[7] In Sissinghurst's defence, it is worth noting that it was quite customary, and both Ightham Mote and Knole nearby are evidence, to build service ranges of timber and lathe. Though the bricks for Sissinghurst were almost certainly made on the site, from clay dug in the Lake Field fired in kilns in Roundshill Wood, the number of bricks required must have limited the building's progress, and to re-use the old buildings, or build new timber buildings, was necessary for the servants' quarters.

Previous page *The view south from the tower-roof across the present rose garden and showing the Rondel of grass enclosed by yew hedging. The old wall between the tower lawn and the rose garden is part of the south range of the Tudor house, and it is thought to have been part of a range of buildings connected to the surviving South Cottage. The rose garden was the old kitchen garden when the Nicolsons found it in 1930, and is the most likely site for the garden of the Tudor house. This garden was in intense cultivation for vegetables during the nineteenth century, following a long tradition. As a Tudor country garden it would have been used for growing salads, herbs, fruit and vegetables for the household, with perhaps small rose bowers for the ladies of the house.*

The truth was that Richard Baker had a deadline to keep, for Sissinghurst's most glorious hour, actually three whole days, was approaching, fixed for 15–17 August 1573, when Queen Elizabeth I and her caravan would arrive to stay, on one of Her Majesty's endless perambulations of England. Lord Burghley, the Queen's principal Secretary, grumbled that the journeying in Kent was hard and difficult; the Weald offered 'worse ground than the Derbyshire Peak District'.[8] The Queen came to Cranbrook from Knole, and the townspeople laid a carpet of their famous broadcloth at her feet. Then, with much excitement and galloping outriders dashing to and fro, her progress marked by fluttering pennants and the loud cursings of courtiers whose horses stumbled in the ruts, she continued along the Cranbrook road, through Milkhouse Street, and down a winding, dipping lane to arrive at Sissinghurst's entrance arch. The bailiff ushered the royal company inside, and the Queen dismounted at the tower steps, to be greeted by Richard and Catherine Baker, proffering a welcoming gift of a silver-gilt cup, with Her Majesty's Royal coat of arms held by a lion on the lid.[9] How proud the Sissinghurst community must have been. What feasting and dancing must have disturbed the customary quiet of the summer-dry fields. When the Queen continued on her way Richard Baker accompanied her to his sister Mary Tufton's house at Hothfield, and eventually to Dover, where she knighted him. When he returned home there were undoubtedly more celebrations at Sissinghurst that summer.

The lady who almost certainly enjoyed this occasion hugely, and who probably made it possible, was Sir Richard's sister, Cecilie Baker, the pivotal personage in this Sissinghurst story. She was the great Sir John's daughter, through his second marriage, to Elizabeth Barrett, and was born in 1535. She spent the long summers of her childhood and youth at Sissinghurst, in the old timber house of the de Berhams which was gradually becoming the brick house of the Bakers. When she was nineteen she was married, in St Bride's Church in Fleet Street, to the grandson of Sir John Baker's Sackville brother-in-law, Thomas Sackville. Their wedding year was 1554, that first nervous year of Queen Mary's reign; both their fathers were powerful men, with estates in Kent and Sussex and property in the City of London; it was a good match. It was also a great tribute to the Bakers' family qualities that Cecilie earned her young husband's respect and retained his affection throughout his meteoric rise to fame. Thomas Sackville, poet and courtier, was cousin of the Virgin Queen; in 1567 he was created Lord Buckhurst and the following year he was Ambassador to France. More embassies, a Garter knighthood, the Chancellorship of Oxford University and the gift of Knole followed before he became Lord High Treasurer and Lord High Steward of England. King James I created him Earl of Dorset in 1604, and he collapsed and died at the Privy Council table four years later. It was, even by Elizabethan standards, a colourful life, and Cecilie accomplished it all with dignity. She became mistress of Knole, and founded the Sackville and Dorset dynasty, which after thirteen generations produced Vita Sackville-West.

Sissinghurst, not yet dubbed a castle, remained the great house of the Bakers for just over one hundred years after Queen Elizabeth's visit. Sir Richard Baker lived quietly and happily amongst his tapestried galleries, with enormous fires and some good (smuggled) French brandy to keep him warm in winter, and surrounded by his flower strewn meadows and orchards in summer. He died in the miserable year of 1594, long remembered for its cold summer and poor harvest. His only male heir, his son John, survived him by just two years, and John's son, Henry Baker (who purchased a baronetcy) lived until 1623. Sissinghurst was now far removed from the dangerous and glamorous life of the Court; it was a little domestic world of its own, governed by the seasons, and surrounded by the agricultural regime that filled its barns, granaries and oasthouses. Sir Henry's heir, his son John, was only fifteen years old when he inherited the estate, but he grew up to be High Sheriff of Kent and Member of Parliament for Hastings. It was this Sir John who pleaded for a royal licence to allow Sissinghurst its own chapel and chaplain, because the rutted track to Cranbrook was too difficult for the household to manage regular church worship. This was granted in 1639, and it is thought that the Priest's House was either adapted or built as the residence of the chaplain, set apart from the main house.

Peaceful times appear to have dulled the Bakers' instinct for survival; Sir John, who supported King Charles I's royalist cause in his youth, was eventually caught on the wrong side and impeached by Parliament. In March 1644 he pleaded as a Recusant for Amnesty, and although he was left to return to Sissinghurst in peace, he was heavily fined and had to mortgage some of the estate. He had no son, and when he died in 1653 his widow married again, and as Lady Howard she remained in charge of Sissinghurst until her death in 1693. During these forty years, with no male heir and thus no future, Sissinghurst fell into neglectful decline. Sir John's daughters all married elsewhere, and when their mother died they inherited a divided property. Their first attempt was to try and find a use for it, and to make some money by advertising the qualities of the water from a chalybeate spring in the park, to the north-west of the house. These springs are not uncommon in this part of Kent (there is one at Scotney Castle) but the promoters of 'Sissinghurst Spa' tried to make out that its waters were approved as better and richer in minerals that those of Tunbridge Wells, the most famous spa of the day. The attractions of Sissinghurst were enthusiastically listed on an advertisement published in 1695: a park seven miles around, well wooded with an open common 'much in use for Horse-racing', three good inns in Milkhouse Street, a cherry garden and plenty of other orchards, with cider selling at sixpence a bottle. The speculation seems largely for the benefit of the local innkeepers, and others with houses to rent in Cranbrook and Milkhouse Street, but a note also records that 'the Gentry' to whom Sissinghurst belonged, were willing to accommodate guests in furnished or unfurnished quarters. The chapel was advertised as an additional amenity.

Whether Sissinghurst's lovely galleries sank so quickly to the level of a lodging-house is uncertain. Nothing much could have come from the spa speculation or it would have appeared in histories; it would certainly have been noted by the hawk-eyed Celia Fiennes, who passed by Sissinghurst on her Kentish journey in 1698, but does not mention the place. On Lady Howard's death Sissinghurst itself, the house and garden, was inherited by her grandson Edmund Hungate Beaghan, and in turn by his five-year-old son, George Edmund Beaghan, who was born in about 1750. Horace Walpole, in his letter to Richard Bentley of 9 August 1752, described the child's inheritance as 'a park in ruins and a house in ten times greater ruins', though, as has already been quoted, Walpole also admitted that vestiges of former beauty were still discernible. The Trustees of young George Edmund Beaghan let his unwanted house to the government, who found a convenient use for it as a prison, from 1756 to 1763, during the Seven Years' War. It was thus as *le château* of its wretched French prisoners of war that it acquired the name Sissinghurst Castle: not a castle of defence against an enemy, but a stronghold to contain them.

If the feasting and dancing for Queen Elizabeth I had been the moment of Sissinghurst's glory, these seven years plumb its saddest and most miserable depths. It was vandalized by everyone; the authorities bricked up the arches, reduced the mullioned windows to slits and tacked up every conceivable kind of lean-to against its inner walls to provide some kind of shelter for anything from 1500 to 3000 souls, and their keepers. Edward Gibbon, a young officer of the garrison who was from a local family (and was to write *The History of the Decline and Fall of the Roman Empire*), recoiled in horror at the 'inconceivable dirtiness' of the place, and the inabilities of an ill-equipped and short-

Below *The corner of the tower lawn where the Lion Pond, which was made by the Nicolsons, was sited; this was the only formal water feature in the garden but the water stagnated so it was filled in. This close-up shows just how the fabric of Sissinghurst suffered from rough treatment over the years. The bricks, made of clay from the lake field and fired in kilns in Roundshill Wood, are crumbling and pock-marked. This particular spot is naturally damp and shady and has been much patched and roughly mortared. Even though Sissinghurst was never of the finest craftmanship, as Hampton Court Palace or Sutton Place in Surrey, it was its appalling treatment – which began in the mid-seventeenth century and only ended with the Nicolsons' restoration in the nineteen-thirties – which makes it look so battered. The lead tank with its pattern of Tudor roses, filled with striking* Fuchsia tryphylla *is lovely recompense. (August)*

handed garrison to cope with too many high-spirited prisoners – 'These enemies, it is true, were naked, unarmed prisoners; they were relieved by public and private bounty; but their distress exhibited the calamities of war, and their joyous noise the vivacity of their nation'.[10] The local people, long in league with French smugglers, found prisoner-relief to their profit and liking. The prisoners sold them things they made – Vita later bought a shield with the Baker arms which had been painted by one of the inmates, and she knew of other ornamental objects, including a full-rigged model ship. From the list of damages to the Castle (as it can now be called) after the government's tenancy, it also seems likely that both jailed and jailors bartered removable artifacts to provide them with more immediate comforts. At the end of the seven years over two hundred yards of panelling had been stripped from the gallery (all that *genteel grotesque* decoration which Walpole had referred to), marble fireplaces had disappeared and every pane of glass was broken; 'not even a rump of a shrub or tree' was left in the garden.[11]

This wreck, released from mortgage in lieu of repairs for damages, was returned to the Beaghan heirs who, quite understandably, had little use for it. Some of the Baker land had already been sold by the heirs of another of Sir John's daughters to the Mann Estate. The Manns of Linton, near Maidstone, now acquired Sissinghurst Castle and its farm for just over £12,000; by this stage the wreckage was fair game, and the Bakers' clock was removed from the tower to adorn the stable block at Linton (where it remains). The Manns were a distinguished family, but none of them cared for Sissinghurst; they had bought it in a ruinous state, merely for the value of its land. When the artist Richard Godfrey arrived to draw the historic castle for illustration in Hasted's *History of Kent*, which was published in 1790, he was just able to discern enough to imagine how splendid the Bakers' house had been. After that it seems that whenever building materials were required, Sissinghurst was plundered. T. D. W. Dearn's *Account of the Weald of Kent*, published in 1814, despaired that little remained except the great entrance range, and the tower itself as a sad relic, shorn of its turret roofs and its clock.

However, Sissinghurst's fortune improved when in 1794 the Mann Estate let the ruins and the farm to the Cranbrook Poor Relief Trustees. These twenty-one burghers of Cranbrook (whose names are on the wall of the Vestry Hall in Cranbrook, which they built with their profits) managed Sissinghurst well as a means of employment and shelter for one hundred poor men and their families. They began to prosper, for during the years 1813–18 the farm's profits yielded £1000 annually for the town's rate relief. Then agricultural depression struck this part of rural Kent, as it did the rest of England, and though Sissinghurst avoided starvation riots, the days of profit were over and there was certainly no money for the repair or restoration of the buildings. Undoubtedly any of the remnants of fine carvings or finished stones that might have remained in place were now too much of a temptation, and the last pieces were spirited away. The parish gave up the farm in 1855; Sissinghurst was known locally as the 'Old Cow' and had been milched of her last drop of usefulness. The Mann Estate devolved, through the female line via Catherine Mann who married the 4th Earl of Cornwallis, to be the Cornwallis Estate, and Sissinghurst became part of the inheritance of the 5th Earl. Lord Cornwallis put in a tenant farmer, George Neve, who was the last to abandon the old ruins. He built himself a substantial farmhouse in purplish brick, with stepped brick gables and pretty Gothic windows, and inside, a fine galleried hall and panelled staircase. He was an important local figure and ran the farm successfully until 1903, when the Cornwallis Estate decided to sell off the property.

Whilst George Neve got on with farming and building his new farmhouse, the late nineteenth-century passion for the antique, and for colourful legends took possession of the old Castle. An amateur antiquarian, Charles Igglesden, who made a series of

The moat wall on the south side of the present orchard. This wall must be, along with the gable arches flanking the entrance, the oldest surviving structure at Sissinghurst and is in the right position to be part of the medieval manor house which stood on the eastern half of the orchard, surrounded by a moat. The moat survives on the north and east sides and a possible third arm is now a grass path known as the moat walk. The wall in this photograph was probably re-used to support timber buildings that were part of the servants' quarters of Sir Richard Baker's Tudor house. When the Nicolsons came in 1930 it was almost completely buried in rubble and overgrown with brambles. (October)

Cotinus coggyira *glows in the October light against the fragile ghost of the end of the moat wall. This wall is the remains of the medieval, moated manor house of the de Saxingherstes and de Berhams, the first Norman families to be recorded as living at Sissinghurst. When Vita discovered this wall whilst clearing the rubbish from the garden in 1930 she was intrigued and enchanted with its antiquity. It was excavated and restored as an ornamental garden feature, and its parallel walk was named after it. It was always to be lightly decorated with flowers through the seasons – wallflowers in early spring, the white wisteria in May and June, and mauvy-blue michaelmas daisies at its feet at the end of summer. The lead vases which ornament its top at discreet intervals were bought from Bert Crowther, the dealer in garden ornaments, one at a time, in the nineteen-thirties. (October)*

'Saunters Through Kent' for the *Kentish Express* newspaper, resurrected and em-broidered Sissinghurst's legends. Sir John Baker, Queen Mary I's Chancellor of the Exchequer, father of the noble Cecilie Sackville, became 'Bloody Baker', the man who had an appetite for local maidens who, once de-flowered, were slaughtered and buried under Sissinghurst's staircases. Igglesden's artist, one Mr X. Willis, sketched the ivy-clad entrance arch and the overgrown pond and gave them a suitably sinister air; the Castle's position amongst trees and far from the road, had always invited the descriptions 'unpleasant' and 'secluded', and now perhaps the malevolent ghosts had taken over, as no one else seemed interested, or cared for the once lovely Castle. Sir John Baker was adopted as the local villain that every country community must have and his shadow fell over the whole of Sissinghurst. This was a pity, for Charles Igglesden also uncovered a rather nicer legend – that Queen Elizabeth I's footprints, made across the soil of the courtyard on that royal visit in the summer of 1573, refused to disappear and could be seen glowing on moonlit nights.

Almost three hundred years later, on a fine noonday in July 1873, Sissinghurst's ruins were finally consigned to antiquity when their historic status was recognized by a visit from the elite Kent Archaeological Society (of whom Sissinghurst's owner, Lord Cornwallis, was a notable patron).[12]

In 1903, when the Cornwallis Estate sold off Sissinghurst, it was the land and the substantial Victorian farmhouse which were the chief assets; the ruins were classed as out-buildings, rather less useful than the barn and its attendant oasthouses. For over twenty years Sissinghurst Castle Farm was owned by Mr and Mrs Barton Cheeseman; during that time they quite naturally befriended their newly arrived neighbours across the field to the north at Bettenham Manor, Captain Oswald and Dorothy Beale. In 1923 Mrs Cheeseman became godmother to the Beale's son John, an event which introduced the Beale family to the Sissinghurst story, where they are to play such a prominent part. Mr Cheeseman died in 1926 and Castle Farm was bought by William Wilmshurst, one of a large and notable Goudhurst farming family; two years later William died, and his son decided to put Sissinghurst back on to the market; and there it stayed, 'poor Sissinghurst! It was greatly fallen.'[13]

THE NICOLSONS
AT HOME

Throughout 1929, the year Britain voted in Ramsay Macdonald's government and Wall Street crashed, Sissinghurst Castle mouldered away. Oswald Beale at Bettenham Manor, much too conscientious a farmer to let good land go sour, quietly worked some of Castle Farm's fields. And farther west in Kent events slowly conspired towards the Castle's fate.

In the village of Sevenoaks Weald, just south of Sevenoaks, a farm named Westwood changed hands; the new owner (whose name is not recorded and who is dubbed a villain in this story) was merely making the best of a doubtful future for agriculture when he decided to go in for intensive poultry rearing. The news of the poultry farm and consequent fields full of unsightly, smelly henhouses, came as a shock to the socialite couple who owned a picturesque cottage called Long Barn, and whose garden

Above *Corner of Vita's writing-room in the tower.*
Opposite *The Long Library, filled with the furniture and paintings which belonged to the Nicolsons.*

overlooked these fields. The couple, who were known locally as Mr and Mrs Nicolson, chiefly used the 'cottage' (which had seven bedrooms) in the summer, but they loved it. He was known to be a diplomat and was away a lot, and she was the daughter of Lord Sackville at Knole who published poetry and novels under her own name, V. Sackville-West. Quite what the daughter of Knole (which was rumoured to have a room for every day of the year, if anyone could count them) needed a cottage in the village for was not a question asked by those who knew her, for she was of independent mind and wanted a place of her own for writing and where she could create a garden. More poignantly, it was known that her father, Lord Sackville, had died in January 1928, and Knole had passed to his brother and his American wife; Mrs Nicolson felt cheated and did not like to go there anymore.

The Nicolsons had many diversions; they travelled a lot and had many aristocratic and artistic friends. At this time their particular friends were the architect Lord Gerald Wellesley (later the 7th Duke of Wellington) and his wife Dorothy who was, like Vita, a published poet. The four of them travelled around Europe together and were constantly at each other's houses. In the spring of 1928 the Wellesleys had bought themselves a wonderfully elegant house, pink and Georgian, named Penns in the Rocks, near Groombridge. It had associations with William Penn and an enchanting small park with outcrops of very decorative rocks and carpets of wild flowers. It satisfied perfectly their taste for fine buildings with Romantic historical associations, and prompted a competitive spirit in the Nicolsons who now began to look for something interesting of their own.

Word passed around, and did not have to pass far. Donald Beale, brother of Oswald, was land agent for the Wellesleys, and he told Dorothy Wellesley about Sissinghurst Castle. She drove Vita and her thirteen-year-old son, Nigel, to look at it on 4 April 1930; Vita immediately telephoned to Harold in London, who took their elder son Benedict down to see it the following day. They liked it, which was fortunate, for in the preceding twenty-four hours Vita had fallen completely in love with her ruined castle. She had learnt of the Baker ancestry, and that Sissinghurst had been the home of Cecilie Baker, her own ancestress, and she now knew that she too had come home.

The Nicolsons bought Sissinghurst Castle, the ruins and the farm, for £12,375 in May 1930. It was a turning point in their lives. But what kind of lives did they lead? Who were these people, mad enough or imaginative enough, wealthy enough or plainly foolhardy, who took on this ramshackle ruin of collapsing walls, and sagging roofs, surrounded by mud and rubbish and a garden full of nettles and old cabbage stalks? Their lives are so richly documented elsewhere that this, the story of their Castle, can only summarize the reasons which brought them to Sissinghurst and anchored them there.[1]

James Lees-Milne's two-volume biography of Harold Nicolson breaks at the end of 1929, 'the great divide' in his life.[2] Harold was born in 1886, the son of a diplomat (his biography of his father *Lord Carnock* was published in 1930) destined for diplomacy. He had grown up in embassies in St Petersburg and Paris to a life of constant travelling; while he was at school in England, and then at Oxford, his holidays were always spent in some exotic place that was a temporary home. He joined the Foreign Office in 1909, spent a few sociable years amongst Edwardian house-parties, until he was posted as Third Secretary to Constantinople in 1912; postings to Teheran and Berlin filled the 1920s, and then (with a horrid jolt) in 1926 he faced the fact that he was approaching forty. The 'great divide' was to give up this life and return to a job in London, as a columnist for the *Evening Standard*, which he began on 1 January 1930. There were complex reasons (half a life's reasons) for his decision but *au fond* it had much to do with his longing for a settled home. The challenge of Sissinghurst Castle came just at the right moment because it

The base of the Shanganagh column resting in the orchard, surrounded by a planting of Polygonum affine superbum. *This is a reminder of Harold's Irish ancestry and he brought it back from a sale in Ireland in the late 1930s. He had discovered that the monument had been erected at Shanganagh Castle to mark the Reform Bill of 1832; six years after that, his disillusioned ancestor had added the words 'Alas, to this date a Humbug'. (August)*

Previous page *The South Cottage showing the front door and the sitting room window, with a border of flame coloured daisies in front. The chair remains outside to the right of the door in memory of Harold's favourite place to sit, outside his writing room. The daisies, flame coloured in keeping with the traditional sunset colours of the cottage garden, are Sutton's hybrids (now called* Venidio-arctotis) *developed from the bear's ear daisy (* Arctotis) *and the old Venidium daisy, which assures the bright colours. (August)*

offered a place where he would never have time to be bored, and he could indulge a streak of deeply-rooted atavism, which he attributed to his affection for his uncle, Lord Dufferin and his Irish estate, Clandeboye.[3] This very element of deep-rootedness had been one of the strongest attractions between Harold and Vita, whom he had met in 1910 and married on 1 October 1913. She had been born and brought up at Knole, and 'belonged' to and believed in that great Elizabethan house and its ghosts in a powerful way. Knole's Renaissance riches, its legends of Venetian ambassadors and Cavalier poets, formed her taste and education and immersed her in an imaginative world that had made her, quite understandably, a poet and novelist. She was flamboyant and a little 'wild' and being rich, striking and clever, attracted much public attention. But she did not like the twentieth-century world very much and, having lost her beloved Knole as her inheritance for legal and gender reasons, she too needed a refuge. During the twenties the idea of 'home' for them both was Long Barn; their 'cottage' and its garden spun a silken thread that kept their marriage intact through turbulent years.[4] So the threat of the chicken farm was more than physical, it threatened a refuge that they both loved. Any replacement for Long Barn (which they had found in poor condition and garden-less in 1915) had to pose a bigger challenge, and promise greater reward. Though Harold, wisely, worried about how much it would all cost, they both knew from the outset that Sissinghurst Castle was what they needed. This immediate, joint bond of conviction that they could make a thing of beauty out of their squalid ruin, that the 'redemption of Sissinghurst'[5] was their united cause, was perhaps their greatest resource.

Everyone who dealt with the sale assumed that the Nicolsons would live in the Victorian Castle Farmhouse, at least for a while. They could not have been more wrong. Vita shunned it completely, and preferred The Bull in Sissinghurst village or camping in her ruin for the family visits during 1930. The first priority was the removal of the rubbish, the accumulated domestic debris of over a hundred years of neglect – old lean-to buildings against the courtyard walls, rusty bedsteads, cast-out sinks, broken farm tools, and unaccountably, piles of sardine tins, all buried in rubble, nettles and brambles. Sissinghurst yielded cartloads of scrap iron and many a large bonfire was needed, but amongst the squalor there were treasures – the workmen were strictly instructed to save all fragments of worked stone, remnants of past grandeur, and they discovered the old stone sinks and troughs (to be used for flowers) and there was great joy at the unearthing of a complete stone Tudor fire surround (later installed in the Long Library). Two other great moments were the uncovering of the moat wall, almost completely buried in earth and brambles, whose antique beauty dictated the moat walk and the subtle adornment of purple wallflowers and white wisteria, and the opening up of the entrance arch, which revealed the vista to the tower. Vita's first love was her tower (which had no light, heat or water) where she chose to have her writing-room; one of her earliest plantings at Sissinghurst were the rosemary bushes beside the tower entrance. Their second priority was the South Cottage, which was renovated to provide bedrooms for Vita and Harold, with Harold's writing-room and a sitting-room downstairs. They spent their first night at Sissinghurst camping in the tower on 18 September 1930, and the South Cottage was ready for sleeping in at the beginning of the following December.

During 1930 and 1931 their lives were still based in London during the week and at Long Barn at weekends. More and more visits were made to Sissinghurst to supervise the clearing up, which took all this time, and the first renovations. This was a slow rediscovery of the Castle beneath its neglect, and it was in this way that their plans materialized. Whilst they cleared, they dreamed of how the courtyards would be filled with flowers, how a pleached lime walk would enclose the moat and orchard, how the orchard would be carpeted with gentians beneath blossoms, and how they would create a beautiful lake. They dreamed that they would build a wing across the north side of the entrance court, that somehow it might be connected to the tower, that they would convert the barrack ranges each side of the entrance into galleries . . . and then they came

Above *The Japanese quince,* Chaenomeles × superba *'Knaphill Scarlet', was amongst the first of the plantings at Sissinghurst in 1930 because the colour of its flowers toned so well with the Castle's old bricks. These grow on the wall outside the library door near the standpipe originally used for watering the stone sinks. (March)*

Left *Harold and Vita posing self-consciously on the steps of the tower for a photograph by one of their sons in the summer of 1933. The photograph catches the atmosphere of the quiet gardening weekends which they loved, hoping to be left in peace and not disturbed by casual visitors.*

When this aerial photograph was taken in July 1932, the Nicolsons had owned their Castle for two years; the walls bear the marks of buildings that have been demolished, the entrance court has been cleared, levelled and grassed, but as yet has no paving. The South Cottage garden and the Priest's House garden have been laid out and the yews of the hedge that is now the double Yew Walk have been planted.

Opposite *Vita's writing-room in the tower: this room and its fittings – virtually as they are seen today – was established as Vita's lair almost as soon as the Nicolsons bought Sissinghurst.*

down to earth and realized that they would have to make best use of what was there already. New buildings of any size were out of the question financially, and so the unconventionality of Sissinghurst as a home was born out of necessity. As long as there was somewhere for Harold and Vita to write in peace, and for their two sons, Benedict and Nigel, to sleep when they were at home, then that was enough; the garden was given the highest priority and having spare rooms for visitors or grand rooms for entertaining was not important. After the South Cottage was made habitable the builders tackled the seventeenth-century Chaplain's house, now known as the Priest's House, which provided a bedroom for the boys and a kitchen and dining-room, which was the realm of the Nicolsons' indispensable housekeeper, Mrs Staples. With this accommodation they moved from Long Barn on 9 April 1932.

The redemption of Sissinghurst was to be achieved within the next five years, and as anyone who has restored or made even the smallest garden will understand, they were five years of hard work. The Nicolsons were both rather obsessed with their new garden

and they made something of a family enclave of their ruin, right from the start. This was observed by James Lees-Milne, who was driven over to visit them by a friend that first August: 'The two Nicolson boys were bathing in the lake. Their clear voices echoed across the water. "Oh, what a bore, here are visitors!"'... Harold and Vita had finished their writing for the day. In spite of the heat they were both bending over a flower border, he in short sleeves and an old panama hat with a black ribbon, she hatless and wearing a drab cotton skirt.'[6] It is not difficult to imagine that they too cursed at being disturbed, but not aloud.

In both James Lees-Milne's biography of Harold and in Victoria Glendinning's *Vita* the years 1932 to 1937 are crammed with activity, and it is easy to understand why, when they did have some time to devote to the garden, the Nicolsons were not pleased at being disturbed. Harold spent six months of that first summer at home, writing *Public Faces* (1932) and *Peacemaking 1919* (1933); Vita wrote *Family History* (1932), in which the tumbledown Sissinghurst features as the home of her hero. Books, journalism and broadcasting were Harold's only source of income and he worried that they did not earn him enough; they packed a lot of garden-work into those months and felt frustrated that they could not afford for things to move faster. Apart from sapping their money and their energies, Sissinghurst revealed some of its less attractive aspects, which they worried about a great deal at this time, and which can be seen in the aerial photograph taken that first summer, in July 1932 (page 26). One worry was the awkward coffin-like shape of the entrance court, which compared so badly with the elegant rectangle of the Green Court at Knole. Vita dreamed of paving the whole court, but they could not afford that, and so her 'precious sweep' of paving from the entrance to her tower was the compromise. The equally coffin-like tendency of the old kitchen-garden, shown in the left-hand side of the photograph, was somewhat alleviated by sectioning off the cottage garden with a simple crossing and four main flower beds. Here at least they could garden in peace and quiet, and undoubtedly the cottage garden was the most rewarding of the earliest projects.

The single yew hedge, which can be seen in the photograph, planted in such a straight line from the old kitchen garden wall to enclose the tower lawn and the Priest's House garden, was Harold's first brilliant stroke of garden-making that summer. Vita called him an 'architect *manqué*'; he had a deep love and knowledge of classical art and architecture but perhaps he had learned more about the way to treat Sissinghurst from his observations – which almost amounted to hero-worship – of Edwin Lutyens at work, and the way his gardens were tightly controlled by vistas and enclosing walls and hedges. Lutyens's Arts and Crafts gardens in England, notably Folly Farm in Berkshire, were rather nearer Sissinghurst's scale than Versailles or Villa d'Este, but Harold was a compulsive garden visitor and it was very much from staring down vistas, English and foreign, that he had learned his 'good eye', which he could now use at Sissinghurst.

In those five years, 1932 to 1937, the garden was made in rather frenetic snatches of inspiration, which had been given much thought on long train journeys or with that acute perspective of the mind which a far away place affords. Both Vita and Harold spent the first three months of 1933 on a hectic lecture-tour of the United States; Harold made three more trips across the Atlantic during 1934 and 1935 in connection with his book on Dwight Morrow. They both, together or with someone else, made at least annual trips to Europe – Vita to Portofino in Italy, Harold to Stockholm, and the family went on a cruise around the Greek islands in the spring of 1935. Harold was a regular reviewer for the *Daily Telegraph* books page, and also wrote his book about Lord Curzon at this time. Vita, having become a best-selling novelist with *The Edwardians* (which had sold 20,000 in its first three months in 1930) produced *All Passion Spent* (1931), *Family History* (1932), two books of short stories (1932), *The Dark Island* (1934), and her *Collected Poems* were

published in 1933. Benedict and Nigel both progressed from Eton to Balliol College at Oxford and spent their long holidays at home, often with friends. Sissinghurst in the making was much enlivened by the turbulent interest of Vita's mother, Lady Sackville, who was either sending them generous gifts of money for plants or beautiful things for the house and garden, or being bitter and disparaging about their efforts, their Bohemian lifestyles and their obstinacy in their devotion to this unlikely ruin. A rather calmer presence, dearly loved by all the family because she would come, and not need entertaining, was Sibyl Colefax. Lady Colefax's presence must have left some kind of blessing on Sissinghurst because of her own exquisite taste, and because she introduced two of her friends, Norah Lindsay and Constance Spry, both gardening ladies whose tastes Vita admired.

It was always Vita's contention that they did not have any real professional help with Sissinghurst, but this must be the case with many delusions of self-sufficiency that garden-makers enjoy. Whilst Harold was undoubtedly the genius 'with square-ruled drawing paper, india-rubber, control of temper, stakes and string' of the design, and she

The moat walk in spring; Vita was as passionate about the careful conservation of the medieval brickwork of this wall as she was about the interior walls of the South Cottage and her tower. She kept her bedroom walls as bare bricks, so that she could enjoy them, with just one or two tapestry hangings. She felt that this moat wall also needed little decoration, merely the most delicate touch of plants, the wallflowers Erysimum linifolium *'Bowles' Variety', to be followed by the white Japanese wisteria. The azaleas are the sweet-scented* Azalea pontica, *with an orange hybrid that remains from Vita's earliest planting. (May)*

was the gardener, it was not true that they managed entirely alone.[7] From August 1932 until his death in May 1936 they were helped by the architect member of the Powys brothers, Albert Powys, usually known as A. R. Powys, who was Secretary to the Society for the Protection of Ancient Buildings at the time. Little is known of how Powys came to advise the Nicolsons, or why they did not choose one of their many architect friends – Gerald Wellesley, Oliver Hill or Geddes Hyslop. Powys was most experienced in matching the time-worn materials of the Castle; he worried and worked for the Nicolsons far beyond simply earning his fees, and exerted an avuncular fussiness over their project which tended to drive Vita into a fury. He planned the major conversion of the Priest's House, he turned the old stables into the Long Library, he built the rose garden's semi-circular west wall and the north wall enclosing the entrance courtyard, and he attended to many of the small details which made the remnants of the Castle look a harmonious whole rather than a patched ruin. But he could not resist giving his opinions on the garden, on the design of the Rondel in the rose garden, on the yew walk and on the levels and paving of the entrance courtyard, and by no means all his suggestions were rejected. But with three 'designers' on the job, who was doing the work? During the Nicolsons' comings and goings, frantic gardening sessions and lengthy absences, their three gardeners carried on quietly as instructed. Two labouring gardeners, George Hayter and his son, had come with the Castle; they cleared the rubbish and dug over the new flower beds, and helped with building-restoration work when required. The building work itself and the laying of garden pavings was all done under the supervision of Dick Beale, Donald Beale's nephew, who had recently joined the family building firm in Tunbridge Wells. It will be remembered that the Nicolsons found Sissinghurst because of Donald Beale, the land agent in Crowborough, whose brother Captain Oswald Beale farmed Bettenham Manor. Vita had soon persuaded the Captain to take over Castle Farm's fields, and she eventually, with difficulty, persuaded Oswald and Dorothy Beale to come and live in the Castle Farmhouse; she was therefore rather delighted to find that this 'happy family game' could be played even farther by employing Beale the builder.

In November 1935, at the General Election, Harold achieved his great ambition and won the seat of West Leicester for the National Labour Party; designing his garden had fortuitously fitted into years of writing and travelling, when he really felt he did not have quite enough to do. Vita's mother, the volatile Lady Sackville, died in early 1936, which was – all things considered – 'a relief', and in her Will she left valuable ornaments to the garden. By the spring of 1936, therefore, the structure of the house and garden was virtually completed and Sissinghurst's combined assets were looking rosier, bolstered by a legacy from Lady Sackville. Planting could begin in earnest. A new gardener, Gordon Farley, started in May and he was to be a great success; there was also an energetic under-gardener named Kenelly, whom Vita liked very much, but at the end of the summer she had to dismiss him for fighting. At Sissinghurst, as everywhere else, there were continuing domestic upheavals.

Though they had been planting right from the beginning and had made many mistakes and suffered losses, the Nicolsons rather prided themselves on their restraint; much of Sissinghurst's success was that the framework was sound, the lawns were well made, the borders were thoroughly cleaned, dug and manured, and the tiny hedging plants were put in, all before too much other planting – which so often compromises efforts – was done. But once planting started they were enthusiastic and lavish in their acquisitions. By this time Vita had a thorough knowledge of nurseries, and what they would provide, and how good they were; she was an avid sender for lists and catalogues and she often discovered a good new nursery or supplier long before others – she had a nose for such things. She also had four particular local Experts (with a capital E) nearby, who became her regular callers and suppliers. She had known the nurseryman and alpine expert Colonel Charles Hoare Grey at Hocker Edge Nursery on the Goudhurst road, since her Long Barn days, and he supplied many treasures and gave her a lot of good advice; Edward Ashdown Bunyard, epicure and rose expert from Allington at Maidstone, was a visitor who amused her, as was Mr W. E. B. Archer, the rose grower from Monk's Horton near Ashford. Finally there was Captain 'Cherry' Collingwood Ingram from The Grange at Benenden, who completes this quartet of horticultural semi-deities who were interested in Sissinghurst's fate.

One of the things Harold said he most admired about Vita was her 'courage to abolish ugly and unsuccessful flowers' and her 'extraordinary taste' in plants.[8] He could not fault her, except over kniphofias (red hot pokers), which she loved and he hated, but otherwise their shared tastes governed the garden. These tastes were anti-Victorian, in keeping with their time, and excluded stiff bedding plants, coarse leaves and rhododendrons. They liked a mix of elegant spires – delphiniums, eremurus, verbascums and all kinds of iris – and colourful carpets of small plants. Harold planted the lime walk in the forties with tiny Persian tulips, rivulets of violas and muscari and hummocks of thrift, saxifrages and primroses. Vita dreamed of a planted pavement crawling with pink daisies, thymes, sedums and pinks, and she planted the tiny flowers that she loved (from memories of happy alpine walking holidays) in the sinks and troughs in the courtyard. She loved plants for historical and literary reasons, and would plant almost anything that was mentioned by Shakespeare. She also loved scented climbers – honeysuckles and clematis – and, above all, she loved old roses.

The young and flourishing garden was first on public show on 1 May 1938, when it was open for charity, for the Nurses' Fund that is now the National Gardens Scheme, for an entry fee of one shilling per person (children free). The sum raised was just over £17. The visitors were enchanted; for local people it must have seemed that the dark ghosts and legends of the old Castle had been truly vanquished. To strangers it must have seemed so unusual, this grand entrance and graceful tower, with the proud flag fluttering on its top, and beyond only two cottages and scattered pieces of open-roofed rooms filled with flowers.

Vita's most successful head gardener, Jack Vass, began work the following year, on 2 October 1939. She was thrilled with him, partly because he was highly recommended by the Royal Horticultural Society and had worked in some grand gardens and now wanted to come to hers, and partly because he was energetic enough to plant one thousand narcissus and one thousand crocuses before 9.30 am on one of his first mornings. But this happy state of gardening affairs could not last in the autumn of 1939, and soon Vass, like every other person of working age, was posted to the War. Vita was left with a community of the very young and the very old, to do what she could. Vass' parting request had been to look after the hedges, even if all else had to be let go. Vita cut them herself, enough to see them through, but almost everything else did go: the Home Guard took over her tower, the army dug themselves into her wood, the lawns and the orchard were grown for hay, the flowers gave way to potatoes, and all her pretty birds flew away, unfed. Sissinghurst, which persisted in blooming bravely in the face of war, lay, with the rest of the Garden of England, vulnerably in the path of invasion and beneath skies full of prowling bombers. For Vita the defence of her little world became her private battle, to be fought by working all day and writing (having carefully checked the blackout) for half the night. Her *Country Notes in Wartime* (1940) and parts of her epic poem *The Garden* (1946) record what it was like. Little more can be said here, except that it was very terrible. Then, in that wonderful, whatever-the-weather, spring of 1945, knowing that

The rose 'Allen Chandler' on the right of the entrance archway inside the courtyard, in flower in late May. Bred by Hugh Dickson in 1924, this climbing rose was one of the first to be planted by Vita at Sissinghurst. (May)

The lime walk photographed by Edwin Smith in the spring of 1963. The main flowering season is over and the last few tulips and narcissi remain amongst seas of forget-me-nots. The limes are those originally planted in 1932. The completely overblown carefreeness of this photograph is typical of the garden in the Nicolsons' day, when they could neither manage – nor did they want – exceptional tidiness at all times. The lime walk is just finishing its performance here, having put on its colourful show from mid-March to late May. Now it can have a well-deserved rest, left in peace until it is tidied, mulched and prepared for the following spring.

Benedict and Nigel were both safely on their way home, she organized a second celebratory opening, on 2 May.

The garden had survived the War with its fabric intact. Jack Vass had thankfully survived too, and applied his energies to a systematic clearing, digging and re-planting of the garden, flower bed by flower bed. It was all to take the best part of five years; the lawns had to be ploughed, levelled and reseeded, and the hedges coaxed back into solidity by careful hand trimming. Harold made it his personal peace mission to restore the polyanthus carpet, 'the company of the bright and the good' in the nuttery, and then to replant his lime walk as a reflection upon his own 'alpine meadow' of a life. One gardener, Sidney Neve, worked for him alone, and Vita and her gardeners never interfered.[9]

The idea of planting white flowers with grey and silver plants in the Priest's House garden, was the result of Harold's wish to keep the garden flowering into July and August for the summer of 1951, the Festival of Britain summer when he felt more visitors than usual would come. The final decision to make the White Garden was Vita's, because white flowers looked so lovely in the dusk, and – as with the scent of the roses that they had first planted – they appreciated this garden at the end of the day, having dinner outdoors whenever possible, or indoors with the door open.

Harold's concern for the Festival visitors illustrates his habitual enjoyment of showing off their garden, especially to his friends. Vita however, became progressively more shy with those she called 'clever' people and was much happier with her garden visitors, her 'shillings', many of whom she got to know well over the years, as they exchanged plants and garden gossip. She was both careless and careful of their presence, according to her mood; many of the visitors in their turn were shy and nervous of intruding – visiting a private garden was a new activity to many in the post war years. Vita could be totally unconcerned, or 'she would accost you, especially if you had a list in your hand, looking imperiously over your arm' and questioning your interest – this is the memory of a devoted 'shilling' of extraordinary artistic talents of her own, Charlotte Osborne.[10]

Mrs Osborne was typical of so many who became accustomed to Vita's presence as a vital part of her garden; once when the Osbornes were leaving without seeing her, she came running out as their car pulled away – 'She cared nothing for conventions or her appearance . . . she thrust her head down to the passenger seat window, nonchalantly using her lipstick while she talked', enquiring if they had enjoyed their visit. 'You *must* come early in the morning or else at evening, it is at its very best at those times', and she meant it. Rarely was admission refused, and the visitors just dropped their shillings into the bowl provided at the entrance, but they never disturbed the peaceful routine life of the place.

Vita began writing her *Observer* column in 1946 and continued for fourteen years with comments upon her gardening and her garden's progress. This was what really made the garden well-known, for so many readers, longing to see the reality, found their way down the lane to the Castle in the middle of the farmyard. So much of the magical spirit of the place was in that element of surprise, of finding this beautiful garden, sitting in a farmyard, at the end of a nondescript lane. The soaring tower was a landmark seen from the road, but there was no gate, no double lodges, not even a name. The garden was walled and hedged securely from straying cattle, but the arch was always open, never gated nor never needed to be, for people were always about. Even in the fifties this was a rather feudal little enclave, a place where the age old traditions of country living were still honoured. 'The mild continuous epic of the soil' which Vita had celebrated in *The Land* (1926) was still the order of the day, even though man had conquered the peak of Mount Everest and was now contemplating reaching for the moon.

As soon as she had discovered Sissinghurst Castle, Vita had set out her intentions in her long poem, simply called *Sissinghurst* (1931); she would retire into country life and take up her birthright 'far from present fashion'. By that she meant the life of her Sackville ancestors, who ran their great estate, but also wrote poetry. During the thirties she had built up her own estate – set out her garden and bought as much of the surrounding land, some seven hundred of the original two thousand acres, as she could afford. During the forties she had fought for it; now, in the fifties, she lived her 'squirish' life to the full and everyone who came to Sissinghurst was enchanted by a sense that the best things of the past prospered here, despite what was happening in the outside world. Other farmers may have been pulling out hedges and making prairies, or fighting urban sprawl and vandalism, but this corner of rural Kent did not have anything to do with such things.

This was not a world of pipe-dreaming nostalgia, falsely buffered from reality; it was an economically viable and efficiently working world. That was what made it good. And it worked because of the remarkable partnership between Vita and her tenant Captain Oswald Beale. The Captain, as he was known, was a perfect foil for Vita's personality; they had a tremendous respect for each other, which grew into affection, and as Vita said, 'never a cross word between us' in all those years, right from the beginning, 1930, until the Captain's death in 1957. Whilst Vita expressed her artistry in her gardening and strode about her domain with her dogs at her heels, a sort of latter day version of her ancestress Lady Anne Clifford or perhaps the famous Bess of Hardwick, the Captain got on with the job of surrounding the garden with its proper setting. He did not suffer fools gladly – but Vita was no fool, especially where the good husbandry of her fields was concerned; her poem *The Land* (too close to the earth for some of her poetic friends) had won the approval of Kentish farming gossip and earned her the epithet 'one of the old school'.

In the Captain, Sissinghurst was fortunate that it found a farmer who also believed in retaining the best of the old traditions. The backbone of Castle Farm was his herd of

The lime walk, a paved path flanked by borders of spring flowers shown here at their peak flowering. Muscari, yellow jonquils, blue and white anemones, the early single tulip 'Apricot Beauty', white double narcissus 'Cheerfulness', a white fritillary and, beyond the terracotta jar, yellow Crown Imperials, Fritillaria imperialis 'Lutea maxima' and further wave upon wave of yellow, pink and white fill the borders. (March)

The White Garden with silver cineraria, white dahlias, and Solanum jasminoides *'Album' climbing over metal arches. This introduction into the White Garden of the spectacular and long-flowering climbing relative of the potato and deadly nightshade is much admired. (September)*

pedigree Guernsey cows, who twice daily ambled from their field to the milking parlour, crossing in front of the Castle entrance, beneath the poplars on their way. To Vita they were part of daily life, and she would drive out at speed in her Jaguar, deftly avoiding the swaying brown and white monsters in her path, but there would be fireworks if the cowman allowed them to nibble her rosemary and stray into the entrance court. The fields around the garden, all with their names (Park Field, the Lake Field, etc) yielded hay, barley, wheat, potatoes, apples and hops in their due season, and the atmosphere at Sissinghurst was governed by this life. Vita had her own small establishment of house-cows, her Jacob's sheep and Abdul the garden donkey and Gracie the garden horse. The house-cows were fed on hay cut from the orchard, their manure treated the roses and they supplied the whole garden community with milk and butter. Castle Farm also contributed to the garden; extra labour could be borrowed for heavy jobs like tree felling, or a tractor relied on to get through the winter snow. In turn, Vita

Delos, with the oasthouses beyond, photographed in September 1989, after an exceptionally hot and dry summer, the sunniest summer of the century. Delos is the corner of the garden between the gateway in the wall by the Long Library and the Priest's House; it was the repository for all the old stones excavated from the Sissinghurst ruins, so named as it reminded Vita of the rocky Greek island when the saxifrages, aubretias and gentians covered the stones. This was particularly effective when scattered with the white blossoms of her favourite myrobalan plum trees, Prunus cerasifera, which were also planted here. The stones were cleared and need for the foundation of the gazebo and the planting changed to mainly shrubs in the early 1970s.

had a deep sense of involvement in the land and walked the fields daily with her dogs, keeping her eyes open for holes in the fencing or signs of intruders. This nicely balanced, busy country life was the background to the garden (it could not have been made in isolation, nor would have been) and was epitomized in the Sissinghurst Flower Club, a modest local duty which in the mid-1950s was proud to acknowledge Lady Nicolson as its President (Harold was knighted in 1953) and the Captain as Chairman.

The end of this enchanting world came with the Captain's death in January 1957. Harold and Vita were away on a winter cruise, and were shattered when the news reached them. 'I can scarcely bear to think of Sissinghurst tonight . . . never was there a man I honoured more, and you know I loved him too . . .' Vita air-lettered to Dorothy Beale. Harold wrote an elegant tribute for the local papers and noted how stunned Vita was, and how she kept repeating' . . . It can never be quite the same again . . .'. Cranbrook Church was packed for the Captain's funeral with hundreds of local people who knew of Sissinghurst in their daily lives, not only for the garden but for this stalwart of the Kentish farming scene – 'the kind of backbone Englishman that poets write about'.

The tenancy of Castle Farm remained in the Beale family after the Captain's death; it was jointly held by his daughter Mary and her husband Stanley Stearns, who managed the farm, the Captain's son, John, a research physician, and his wife Rosemary who lived at Sissinghurst, as they still do. The pattern of farming and gardening continued in its quiet way until Vita's death. She died in the early afternoon on 2 June 1962, in the bedroom of the Priest's House with the window that overlooked the White Garden. Her cousin, Eddie Sackville-West, now Lord Sackville (who had already transferred Knole to the National Trust) knew how things were when he wrote to Evelyn Irons '. . . it is all very sad, and one wonders what on earth will happen to that lovely garden. As long as Harold lives, I suppose it will continue the same . . . but people's gardens are apt to die with them, even if the status quo is kept – or perhaps just because of that'.[11]

SISSINGHURST
AND THE
NATIONAL TRUST

For a while, outwardly at least, things did remain the same. Harold, though 'horribly unhappy', struggled on in an effort to maintain his routine. After Vita's death he lost his sense of purpose and found very little pleasure in life. Nigel and his wife Philippa and their children came to live in the wing on the right of the entrance arch, which had been specially converted for them, while Harold kept to the South Cottage and spent his time pottering in his garden. Gradually he grew more absent-minded and more frail, until he needed much of Philippa's love and support. He was eighty in November 1966 and enjoyed his birthday celebration, but a few months afterwards he gave up his Albany apartment in London and retired to Sissinghurst; he died there on 1 May 1968.

Behind the scenes, and in consultation with their father when he had felt up to it,

Opposite *The White Garden with the Virgin among foxgloves and columbines, photographed in June.*
Above *The vista from the tower lawn to the entrance arch. (August)*

Nigel Nicolson at the door of the gazebo, his little writing-room which looks out over the Kent countryside. This was a favourite view of his father's and he and his brother had the gazebo built, to the design of Francis Pym, as a memorial to Harold in 1969. Nigel, who has been soldier, politician and publisher in his time, now writes biographies and books on military history, architecture and travel.

Opposite *The wing on the right, south side, of the entrance arch at Sissinghurst which is Nigel Nicolson's private home; he came to live here permanently after his mother's death. He and his elder brother, Benedict, agreed that Sissinghurst should go to the Treasury in lieu of death duties on the understanding that it would be passed into the care of the National Trust, as it was in April 1967. The roses that wreathe the walls are the climber 'Meg', with clusters of pink flowers, and the creamy Rosa wichuraiana 'Gardenia'. (June)*

Benedict and Nigel had had to make some decisions. Vita's will had left Sissinghurst to Nigel, and equivalent property to Benedict, and £45,000 in Estate Duty tax was levied on her legacy.[1] They felt there were two courses open to them; in order to keep the Castle and the garden they would either have to sell the surrounding farmland to pay the death duty, or they could hand over the entire property to the Treasury in lieu of the duty on the understanding that it would be transferred into the care of the National Trust. The first course, they felt, ran the risk of Sissinghurst being surrounded by an unsympathetic type of farm management, or, at worse, building development. The second course was well tried; it had been made possible by the establishment of the Land Fund by the Chancellor of the Exchequer, Harold's friend Hugh Dalton, in 1946. The National Land Fund was used to re-imburse the Revenue for properties accepted in lieu of death duties; Cotehele in Cornwall was the first house to pass to the Trust in this way in 1947. There were three conditions for this step to be possible – the property had to be important enough, in historical terms, it had to be open to the public and to be financially self-supporting.

Nigel has written that he and his brother 'agreed without hesitation' to adopt the second course open to them and make Sissinghurst over to the National Trust. But how did the heirs to Sissinghurst feel about the place they had inherited? They had come to the Castle, a ruin, as teenagers, none too happy at Eton, and for both of them it must have been something of a holiday lark. They had seen it change, in sudden spurts, on visits home from Oxford, from the War and now in peace-time. Benedict was single-minded in his career; he had taken a path that suited his talents, via Bernard Berenson at Villa I Tatti outside Florence, the American and London art worlds, and had been appointed (much to Vita's pride) Deputy Surveyor of the King's Pictures and relinquished this honour (much to Vita's chagrin) to become editor of the *Burlington Magazine* in 1947. He was acknowledged by everyone to be a brilliant, generous, if unconventional, art historian and he was to make the *Burlington* the most respected voice on its subjects in the world. He was like his mother, and his talents were similar to hers; consequently he was at war with her. In August 1955 he married the Italian art historian, Luisa Vertova, and their only child, Vanessa, was born the following year. Luisa spent much of her time at Sissinghurst whilst she was pregnant and whilst Vanessa was tiny; she observed the bitterness of the battle: 'it used to upset me no end, to watch Vita's efforts to start a pleasant talk with Ben and Ben snapping at her . . . he seemed to relish to treat her as a Philistine, an idiot about art history; but his scorn was obviously rooted in some deep need to destroy in his mother a romantic view of himself'.[2] Luisa, and who can know better, attributes Benedict's antagonism to a fairly conventional revolt against his background, and the influence of his friends towards a (then) highly fashionable pacifism, the now recognised 'Brideshead Revisited' philosophy of dying for one's friends rather than for one's country. Luisa knew that Benedict 'must have realized the poetic quality of Sissinghurst' and its beauty, 'but never never said so'. He gave himself away though, for she adds: 'his real answer to his mother's creation of Sissinghurst' was in his writings on art history, with 'the same scholarly precision, insight, imagination and poetic language Vita could master when dealing with her garden or writing about gardening'.[3] His monograph on Joseph Wright of Derby which is so highly regarded, certainly bears this out: 'he loved above all, the off-beat and the provincial' and in this book especially he relishes the scenes and characters of Midlands prosperity and pride upon which Joseph Wright based his reputation. Above all, as an art historian, he had that inherited 'sharp, uncanny awareness of quality' – which of course, Vita had with her flowers.

Nigel, the younger by two and a half years, was more like his father, and had his father's interests in politics, history, literature and architecture. He had become George

The view towards the cottage garden photographed in early April 1989. This was a familiar view to Harold, especially in his last years when he lived in the South Cottage all the time, and where he died on 1 May 1968. This was his particular part of the garden with which he felt an 'elective affinity'. Beyond the clumps of colourful tulips and the sprouting hosta leaves can be seen the pleached lime trees in his own lime walk. In this photograph the garden, in immaculate condition, is awaiting the first opening day of the season and the visitors to come; the guy ropes on the trees are the vestiges of the patient care that was needed to re-establish so many of Sissinghurst's trees which were badly damaged in the great storm of October 1987. (April)

Weidenfeld's partner in the publishing firm Weidenfeld & Nicolson and was elected Conservative MP for Bournemouth East in 1952. Nigel had married Phillipa Tennyson d'Eyncourt and their daughter Juliet was born in 1954, to be followed by Adam in 1957 and Rebecca in 1963. Harold and Vita were softened at the thought of Sissinghurst passing to their grand-children, and in 1956 Vita explained that she was intending to leave Sissinghurst divided between Benedict and Nigel, and that she hoped they would both be able to live at the Castle, at least at the weekends. Benedict, being a thoroughly urban person and unattuned to domestic efficiency, in Luisa's words 'categorically refused'. Vita, trying to soften things a little farther, offered them the old farmhouse at Bettenham, which they accepted and used as their country home for a short while. However, sadly Benedict and Luisa were divorced just after Vita died, and Luisa continued her career and created a home for her daughter in Italy. Nigel and Philippa too were unhappy, though Philippa stayed at Sissinghurst until after Harold's death, as he was very attached to and dependant upon her in his last months. They were eventually divorced in 1970. Benedict did not want to live at Sissinghurst, as he had said, but he accepted a cottage near the Castle, where his daughter Vanessa now lives.[4]

It was therefore largely up to Nigel, with his brother's acquiesence, to handle the transfer to the Trust, on the condition that he and his heirs could continue to live in the Castle. At that time it seemed a totally obvious and natural solution. Harold had been so closely associated with the National Trust since the War, and he had always been interested in its work. It was an organization that involved his oldest and closest friends, James Lees-Milne and Eardley Knollys, Gerald Wellesley, now 7th Duke of Wellington, and his neighbour, Christopher Hussey who lived at Scotney Castle. Harold had enjoyed his National Trust work most of all; he had been on the Historic Buildings Committee under Lord Esher's Chairmanship, and had been Vice-Chairman of the Executive

Committee for fourteen years, working with the Earl of Crawford and Balcarres, and he had only resigned from the Trust the year before Vita's death. Some of the houses they most admired, Sir Walter and Lady Jenner's Lytes Cary in Somerset, Lord Curzon's Bodiam Castle in Sussex and Eddie Sackville-West's Knole, had passed into its care. In Trust ownership the status quo was virtually preserved; it was 'the extension of a private world'[5] and many of the people Harold knew and liked had complete confidence in it.

If anyone heard Vita's voice crying out, repeating her reply to Nigel when he had broached the question ten years earlier, nothing was said – 'Never never never. *Au grand jamais, jamais*. Never, never, never. Not that hard little metal plate at my door. Nigel can do what he likes when I am dead, but so long as I live no Nat. Trust or any other foreign body shall have my darling. No, no. Over my corpse or my ashes; not otherwise. It is bad enough to have lost my Knole, but they shan't take S/hurst from me. . . They shan't; they shan't; I won't; they can't make me. I Won't, they can't make me, I never would'.[6] In the end, motherly reason overwhelmed the passion of the redeemer of Sissinghurst, and she left a note for Nigel to find after her death to say that she would understand if he gave the garden to the National Trust.

Sissinghurst's orchard on an autumn day. The trees are an old red crab apple, and on the extreme right, the loaded branches of Malus 'Golden Hornet'. the flag, especially ordered by Vita, depicts quarters for Sackville and West – '1st and 4th argent with fesse-dancettee sable' (West) and '2nd and 3rd or and gules la bend vair' (Sackville); today the flag is flown when the garden is open. Of almost equal pride of possession was the clock, which has a face on the west and east sides of the tower parapet and was installed – after strengthening the tower to carry the bell cradle – in the summer of 1949. The original clock was taken away when Sissinghurst was owned by the Mann Estate and is now on the stable block at Linton near Maidstone. (October)

Sissinghurst Castle and its farm officially passed into the ownership of the Trust on 17 April 1967. What kind of organization was it? What effect would it have on Sissinghurst, a modest property in comparison with the fifty-two staircases and acres of roof of Knole, and a fragile achievement, compared with the classical certainty of Robert Adam's Osterley Park, or even the landscaped acres of Stourhead?

The Trust was founded in 1895 by three perceptive people: Octavia Hill, housing reformer and champion of higher education for women, Canon Rawnsley, who was devoted to the Lake District, and Sir Robert Hunter, a solicitor who loved Surrey. They founded a public company not trading for profit, which would acquire – by purchase or donation – 'beautiful and historic places' that were at risk. They concentrated on land, which is why the National Trust has come to own so much of the Lake District National Park, and modest buildings of interest; the fourteenth-century Clergy House at Alfriston in Sussex was their first property. In 1907 the Trust was incorporated by an Act of Parliament, which effectively confirmed the State's approval of its purposes and judgement, and proposed that its properties be declared 'inalienable', or never sold or mortgaged and protected by all the majesty of the Law. It was still an independent organization but this blessing from on high allowed close co-operation with government departments and paved the way for future progress. The twenties gave rise to the conservation movement and in 1926 the Council for the Preservation of Rural England was founded to fight urban sprawl; meanwhile the Trust concentrated upon land, the coastline and small and old buildings. Everyone assumed that the country houses of England were still safely in the hands of their respective heirs and settled in the hearts of their large estates. It was in 1934 that Philip Kerr, Lord Lothian, who had recently inherited Blickling Hall in Norfolk (along with his title and Scottish properties) and had no heir, suggested that the Trust should be thinking about acquiring country houses. He shocked the Trust's Annual Meeting into the realization that many great houses and estates were crumbling into dereliction, a process which the Second War inevitably confirmed. So when Harold joined the Historic Buildings Committee at the end of 1944, the business of identifying the most important houses at risk was in full swing, and under its new Country Houses Scheme, the Trust was acquiring a stream of impressive, but mostly dilapidated houses. To qualify, these houses had to be of great architectural merit and to be endowed, open to the public, and, in the main, still lived in by their donors and families, so that they seemed like homes rather than museums. The 1946 National Land Fund, which allowed houses to be accepted in lieu of estate duties, was extended in the 1950s to cover the contents of houses so that family collections of pictures and furniture could be kept intact and in their proper settings. In this way the greatest treasures of English country living tumbled into the Trust's capable hands. Among over eighty great houses – which in any other country would be called palaces – amassed by the Trust were the Proud Duke of Somerset's Petworth in Sussex with its unique collection of paintings, Bess, Countess of Shrewsbury's Hardwick Hall in Derbyshire, designed and built by Robert Smythson with 'more glass than wall', the Astors' Cliveden in Buckinghamshire, the Rothschilds' Waddesdon Manor in Buckinghamshire, with its collections of Meissen and Sèvres china, and Castle Drogo in Devon, designed by Edwin Lutyens, as 'the last castle to be built in England'.[7] Into this magnificent company entered little Sissinghurst.

One may well ask how and why this happened. Clearly a very different set of values was at work because even the Castle's rose coloured bricks and the echo of Queen Elizabeth's footsteps could not lift its history or architectural merit into the class of a Hardwick or Petworth. Sissinghurst was acquired in accord with the Trust's original policy of saving small properties of particular historic interest, such as Rudyard Kipling's Bateman's in Sussex, and Ellen Terry's Smallhythe Place near Tenterden in Kent.

Opposite *The path from the tower lawn through to the Rondel garden, with a marvellous high-level flowering combination of* Magnolia liliflora *'Nigra' on the left, a carmine wallflower spraying out from the old wall and one of Sissinghurst's reputedly eighty-five different varieties of clematis, a long-growing resident. Below the magnolia are hybrids of* Primula sieboldii. *It is just this combination of flowers and an exquisite vista that makes this garden such an inspiration to so many visitors; the qualities that Harold explained as just the right balance of expectation and surprise. In the far distance is the Bacchante, the statue at the head of his lime walk. (May)*

Though Vita had written most of her poetry and the majority of her novels, including her most famous, *The Edwardians* (1930), before she came to Sissinghurst, it was her literary reputation – recognized with the award of her Companion of Honour in 1949 – that had cast its aura upon her garden-making. In retrospect, it is also possible to see how important Sissinghurst was as the background, the necessary firm base, for Harold's commentaries on life in mid-twentieth-century Britain, for which he must be the most often-quoted authority. It was his luck, whether diplomatic or political, always to be at the heart of matters, and his particular brand of dilettantism (which made him such a pert and perceptive observer) found a truly eighteenth-century expression, completely in character, in the making of his garden. Sissinghurst was worthy of the Trust's attention for all these reasons, but the chief reason for its acceptance was the garden itself.

The acquisition of a property by the Trust for the sake of its garden was still relatively unusual in the 1960s, and I think it would be fair to add that there was almost no popular understanding or recognition of the concept of conserving gardens at that time. It is well worth recording the growing awareness of garden conservation in England, particularly during the last twenty years, as it has had an undeniable effect on Sissinghurst's development since the Trust acquired it.

The National Trust must be given all the credit for pioneering the idea of conserving gardens in this country. This began immediately after the Second War, when the fate of great gardens was seen to be even more perilously balanced than that of their houses; the first meeting of the Trust's Gardens Committee was on 23 March 1948, with Lord Aberconway as Chairman. It was a combined committee of the National Trust and the Royal Horticultural Society and its members were all great gardeners – the Earl of Rosse, the Hon. David Bowes-Lyon, the Hon. V. Sackville-West, Sir Edward Salisbury and Dr H. V. Taylor. The Committee's purposes were to consider the management of gardens the Trust already owned and to raise money for the acquisition of other gardens on their merits. The most pressing case, which took much of the Committee's time, was that of Hidcote Manor in Gloucestershire, the garden made by Major Lawrence Johnston in the preceding forty years. Major Johnston was ill and wished to retire to his house in the south of France; he had intended leaving Hidcote in the care of his long-time gardening companion and friend Mrs Norah Lindsay, but she had died rather suddenly at the beginning of 1948. Vita was particularly keen that the Trust should take Hidcote Manor, and this was successfully accomplished largely due to her efforts. Indeed the Committee were singularly successful in forwarding their cause, and Lord Aberconway's own Bodnant in North Wales, with its magnificent terraces and woodland glen full of plant treasures – ' one of the greatest gardens in the world' in the opinion of Arthur Hellyer – passed to the Trust in 1949, to be followed by Nymans in Sussex, the extensive and romantic plant-collectors' garden made by the Countess of Rosse's father and grandfather, in 1954. Also in that year the Trust acquired the magnificent Sheffield Park in Sussex, first planned by Capability Brown but greatly and richly endowed with plants by Captain A. G. Soames, who had died in 1948.

Vita was a loyal and hardworking member of the Gardens Committee and rarely missed a meeting, from 1948 up until her last attendance in May 1961. Like herself, the Committee were all great gardeners and certain that their family's influence would continue to be exerted on their own gardens, and that their sympathetic and enlightened care would be lavished on others, so it was the best possible system. They directed the Trust's care, approving all maintenance and restoration schemes; to carry out their wishes in planting terms, in 1954 they appointed a Horticultural Adviser, Miss Ellen Field, who was to report regularly on the planting.

Against this background, it is therefore clearly understandable that Vita – despite her

diary's outburst against the National Trust owning her garden in her lifetime – realized that this Committee of her own kind would know what to do with her garden too. In one way the Gardens Committee was such a familiar institution that she could have complete faith in the unknown future, and in another, she probably privately nurtured the thought that either Benedict and Luisa or Nigel and Philippa would become deeply interested in the garden after she was gone. But it was also part of her complex personality, as Victoria Glendinning has shown in *Vita*, not only to be able to see both sides of any coin at the same time, but also to have persistent blind spots. Undoubtedly throughout the fifties, as she worked for the conservation of other peoples' gardens, she persistently shelved any real concentration upon the future of Sissinghurst. She simply carried on, knowing that things would be different after her death, and that she would not be there to mind. However, it is irresistible to wonder what she did want, even if only

The entrance seen from the tower roof in spring: a few early flowers are beginning on the climbing rose 'Allen Chandler' but the large Ceanothus *'Southmead' is in full flower. (May)*

in the name of those who loved her, and it would be true to say that the strongest of her loyalties was to her family, to the Sackville/Nicolson way of doing things, and her deepest pain was felt when alien tastes besmirched the things she deeply cared about. It was the imposition of tastes that were not her own on both Long Barn and Knole, after she had left them, that hurt her most. Perhaps the only guarantee for her soul to rest in peace would have been if one of her sons had kept Sissinghurst going.

Such feelings as these were certainly kept to herself and in day-to-day living it was best to ignore them. Much more obviously important, especially in the company of her gardening peers on the Trust's committee, was the practical aspect of keeping the garden going and finding the right kind of staff. Everything, of course, depended upon a reliable Head Gardener, and in 1957 the knowledgeable and energetic Jack Vass left Sissinghurst, having spent his ten post-war years entirely remaking the garden and restoring it to a peak of beauty. The difficulty of replacing him preoccupied more of Vita's thoughts than the unknown future of her garden, and the story of the 'succession' has been of signal importance to Sissinghurst.

Sometime during 1959 Vita had heard from two ex-students and lecturers at Waterperry Horticultural School, enquiring if she knew of a likely property, perhaps an old walled garden, that they could buy to start their own nursery. The two young gardeners, Pamela Schwerdt and Sibylle Kreutzberger, had written to a number of people in this way because the advertisement that they had put in the personal column of *The Times* (still then on the front page) was held up in a newspaper strike. Impressed by their approach and their background, Vita asked if they would come to Sissinghurst and consider becoming her Head Gardeners, as Vass's successor Ronald Platt had now given in his notice. Though both sides understood that this was not what they wanted, the young women liked Sissinghurst, and when the advertisement finally did appear, it yielded nothing more attractive, so they began work as Head Gardeners in the autumn of 1959. Though Vita and Harold proudly wrote to each other of their feminist sympathies and enthusiastically about the knowledge and energy of their new staff, the 'Mädchen', as Vita christened them, were a novelty. She was enchanted by what they did and how they did it and by their practical experience with plants, and for several months after their arrival visitors were shown the gardeners, rather than the garden. As fate transpired they just had time to work themselves in before Vita became seriously ill; though she rallied and took more interest in her garden during her final year in 1961, the girls found themselves all too soon and suddenly almost solely responsible for keeping it going. Their thorough professionalism and quiet way of simply getting on with their job was the real reason why the garden went on flowering through the eventful sixties, after Vita's death, whilst its fate was being decided, and when it finally passed to the National Trust in 1967. They were singularly well equipped for this task, two remarkable people who were in the right place at the right time; they are rather particular heiresses to an interesting part of twentieth-century gardening history, and Sissinghurst was an especially appropriate niche for them.

Both Pamela Schwerdt and Sibylle Kreutzberger had gone to study at Waterperry Horticultural School in Oxfordshire in 1949, and after the two year diploma course they had both continued to hold various posts connected with the School. It was a very special place and had been founded by Beatrix Havergal in the 1930s. Miss Havergal had been to an equally distinguished institution, the Thatcham Fruit and Flower School near Newbury, but she ran Waterperry exactly in the way the pioneer of gardening for women, Frances Wolseley, had run her Glynde College for Lady Gardeners during the years before and after the First World War. Lady Wolseley, like Daisy, Countess of Warwick, at her Studley College, believed emphatically that the daughters of the

The White Garden, reduced to its bare bones in early spring. Under the care of the Trust, these paths have been re-laid and the iron arbour for the Rosa mulliganii *has replaced the almond trees which had died and formerly made the centrepoint of the garden. The box hedges, which are still cut by hand, have to be very carefully kept in scale with the small and complex garden as well as in keeping with the plants inside the 'boxes'. Their perfect appearance is a credit to the skills of the gardeners. (March)*

middle-class should be equipped with a worthwhile career opportunity, and they gave a thorough training to enable their students to run their own nursery or become competent head gardeners. The two-year course included the theory and practice of growing everything from carnations to kale, of growing and marketing vegetables, fruit and flowers which were sold in the college shop, and from the planning of day-to-day management of a large garden to the repair of a pane of glass in a cold frame. Miss Havergal demanded excellence of a high order, as Lady Wolseley had done before her, because both of them knew only too well that for a young lady to succeed in a man's world she had to be twice as capable.[8]

Pamela Schwerdt and Sibylle Kreutzberger were very much part of this excellent tradition. They came to Sissinghurst in time to learn about the garden from Vita and Harold, along with the 'old guard' of George Taylor, who had come in 1946 and who patiently cut the hedges by hand, Sidney Neve, whose primary job was to look after the lime walk for Harold, and a young gardener, Gordon Farris. This capable staff carried the garden through the years from Vita's death to its acquisition by the National Trust. Pamela Schwerdt and Sibylle Kreutzberger have been Sissinghurst's head gardeners for over thirty years; they lived there and worked in the garden for as long as Vita did.

But to return to 1967. It was significant that 'little' Sissinghurst came into the National Trust's care at the moment when it had more than enough serious commitments of a more onerous kind. In the sixties the Trust was coping with the burden of all those great houses it sought to save and a vast programme of repair and restoration works. As if this was not enough, it was being bombarded with criticism for apparently forgetting its primary aims, that of saving the landscape of England and Wales. The fascinating politics of the Trust's battles and how they were won, do not belong here; the crucial point was that the outcome of the problems was that the inner workings and commitments of the Trust were subjected to the scrutiny of an accountant, Sir Henry (now Lord) Benson, who, as accountants will, produced a report full of alarms and despondencies, backlogs and shortfalls, arrears in repairs and lack of adequate systems to cope. The consequent re-organization of the Trust abolished the Gardens Committee, the institution Vita had been so fond of, in 1968, just as Sissinghurst came into its care.

At the same time the world outside the Trust was catching up with its enlightened lead and an interest in the conservation of gardens was being born. When Vita died in 1962 there was, in the present meaning, no such subject as garden history. There were, of course, historic gardens (Versailles and Hampton Court immediately spring to mind) but they were rather a different matter. I know of many people who would agree with me that, although there were earlier landmarks (Christopher Hussey's *The Picturesque*, 1927, Dorothy Stroud's *Capability Brown*, 1950 and Barbara Jones' *Follies & Grottoes*, 1953) it was Peter Hunt's *Shell Gardens Book*, 1964 which first ran the whole gamut of the centuries: garden styles, features, gardening people and plants that 'created' the subject. The following year the Garden History Society was formed. Naturally the first garden historians were mostly interested in the seventeenth and eighteenth centuries, the years of the French- and Dutch-style formal gardens and of the English landscape movement. It has taken a while for the interest to spread in both directions, back to medieval gardens and garden archaeology and forwards into more recent times, to Victorian and Edwardian gardens. Alongside the development of an academic subject there has been progress in what may be called 'applied' garden history, that is the identification and restoration of historic gardens. There is a very real fascination in finding only dereliction and decay and then making the flowers bloom again; this has caught the public imagination and a wide-ranging movement has been enthused by the 'before' and 'after' images of well-known restorations – of the careful replanting of the Lutyens and Jekyll

Following page *The herb garden in midsummer; many visitors to Sissinghurst are particularly fascinated by this small garden enclosure above all others. Over one hundred varieties of herbs, familiar and strange, are grown here and carefully tended throughout the summer to maintain the rich contrasts of colour and textures in leaves and flowers. Prominent in this photograph are clumps of lavender cotton, lavender, hyssop and pot marigold. (July)*

garden at Hestercombe by Somerset County Council, of the National Trust's restoration of Claremont Landscape Garden and the seventeenth-century garden of Ham House, both in Surrey, and (the greatest challenge of all) the current efforts to recall Charles Hamilton's picturesque pleasure park at Painshill in Surrey by Painshill Trust. There is now a sympathy for 'old' gardens, for their care and repair, for the old varieties of flowers and fruit which once grew in them and are now revealed as things of value that we have lost; such 'old' plants are now the special concern of the National Council for the Conservation for Plants and Gardens. Gardens that are open, whether regularly or on occasional Sunday afternoons under the National Gardens Scheme are now very conscious of their 'historic' assets and attractions.

This groundswell of interest, which is not unconnected with the general greening of Britain, has been vastly influential for the garden conservation lobby. The Garden History Society have persuaded English Heritage to survey and list historic gardens on a county by county basis in the same way as historic buildings are listed. An historic garden conscience has been formed, defining gardens as of value in themselves, demanding careful research into and recognition of their planting and atmosphere, and treating the historic garden as an equally important element in the landscape as an historic building. The identification of historic gardens has now come forward in time in accordance with the customary thirty-year rule; this means that the best gardens made during the post-war decade have become officially 'historic'. Sissinghurst is registered by English Heritage as a Grade I garden in Kent, the highest accolade denoting its exceptional quality, and is officially ranked in historic value along with the gardens of Penshurst Place, Hever Castle and Knole.

Vita lived to see her garden become famous; in the succeeding decades it has become exceptionally so. The move into the more public realm of the Trust's ownership of Sissinghurst was signalled by the increase in the garden's visitors, from 28,000 to just over 47,000 in the summer of 1967, the first time it was advertised to National Trust members. The following year, the year that Harold died in May and he and Vita were remembered at a joint memorial service in St James's Piccadilly, there was a further increase, and the following year a further 10,000 visitors came. The idea that the visitors, by sheer pressure of numbers, could damage the thing they came to see, was a new and rather shocking revelation. This had been forced upon the Trust dramatically in 1966, not far away at Sir Winston Churchill's home, Chartwell near Westerham. During the period from June till October of that year, the first year Chartwell was open, the rush of visitors had turned every grass path and the large stretches of lawn into quagmires, which the garden consultant Lanning Roper was called in to 'rescue' by laying careful sweeps and edgings of York stone paving. Perhaps wisely, and in anticipation of similar problems at Sissinghurst, it was decided to change the grass paths in the rose garden to brick and York stone and to pave the herb garden paths, which were of concrete 'stepping-stones' covered in grass and thymes. Once the process was started, the old paving looked inadequate and untidy, and all Sissinghurst's pavings were relaid between 1968 and 1971. Also in 1971 the steps from the tower to the lawn were redesigned and rebuilt, and the following year work on the tower roof – never opened to visitors in Vita's lifetime – replaced the lead with pavings. Delos, the 'ever-troublesome' garden between the library and the Priest's House (where the old stones unearthed from the ruins made a kind of rockery) was tidied and planted with shrubs which would grow in the shade of the walls and tolerate the chilly north winds. The stones were used as foundations for the Gazebo, built as a memorial to Harold to the design of Francis Pymn, in 1969.

Nigel asked Anne Scott-James, who was married to the cartoonist Sir Osbert Lancaster and had known Sissinghurst for years, to write the story of the making of the

Dionysus in his beech alcove. All the garden ornaments have made-to-measure canvas coats to protect them through the winter in the care of the National Trust. (March)

garden. She visited Sissinghurst throughout a whole season for her book, which was published early in 1974; in it she has carefully and knowledgeably described the garden's flowering with an admirable richness and profusion, which she felt Vita's *style* inspired. Almost the only thing that worried her was the tendency towards over-neatness – she felt Vita would not have liked to see the courtyard yews tied into stiff cones, something she had steadfastly avoided in her lifetime; she liked them lax and lavish. Anne Scott-James voiced the concerns of many who had known Sissinghurst for years, and she identified just the changes that a large number of visitors had made inevitable – 'Two or three people can duck under a rose bush which meets another rose bush across a path, but a thousand people cannot do so without a bumping of heads. Two or three people can pick their way across a broken piece of crazy paving, but when there is a stream of visitors somebody is sure to twist an ankle'.[9] She mourned the 'utterly delightful' imperfections which a large number of visitors had frightened away; many of us mourn them, but the garden has to be strengthened in such ways to support its growing fame.

During the 1980s more and more people have come to Sissinghurst, and it can probably fairly be called the most-loved garden in the world. In 1986 there were almost 140,000 visitors during the open season, from 1 April to the middle of October, which was felt to be the maximum this small, ten-acre property could cope with. The Trust is very loathe to impose restrictions, such as time limits, on its visitors, and it has been through much thought, vigilance and hard work on the part of the gardeners that the garden remains impeccable. In the endless hot summer of 1989, which will be fondly recalled in England for a long time to come, the garden entertained over 166,000 visitors; where else in the world would this number of people pass without leaving any litter or damage behind them? Many of the photographs in this book were taken during that summer, when the gardeners also had to cope with persistent drought, and yet, as these photographs show, Sissinghurst looked as beautiful in October as it did in May. This is a remarkable tribute to the skills of the head gardeners, Pamela Schwerdt and Sibylle Kreutzberger, who have devoted so much of their time and energy into making Sissinghurst a place of extreme beauty which draws these thousands of visitors. Their careful renewal of the borders of flowers that contribute to Sissinghurst's style, whether in the traditions of the rose garden, the cottage garden or the White Garden, and their inspired variations that give the regular visitors (of which there are so many) refreshment and delight at every season, have formed our present vision of this now famous garden.

Within the last twenty years, Sissinghurst has become a garden that draws visitors from all over the world, and it stands near the top of the National Trust's visitors' league table, along with St Michael's Mount in Cornwall, the landscaped acres of Stourhead in Wiltshire and Sir Winston Churchill's Chartwell. The haphazard parking near the Castle entrance, with visitors wandering in and leaving their money in a bowl on the table, belongs to the past. Instead the Trust has recently constructed a large new car park and picnic area (carefully screened from the garden and with a shop and restaurant occupying the former farm buildings) and the number of people in the garden is accurately monitored by a 'magic eye', which counts visitors in and out of the garden.

Sissinghurst is now managed from the National Trust's Regional Office for Kent and East Sussex based at Scotney Castle; with overall responsibility in the hands of the Managing Agent. The Head Gardeners are responsible for the care and upkeep of the garden, but they are in frequent touch with the Trust's Gardens Advisory Office. From 1967, the year Sissinghurst came to the Trust, until 1985 the Adviser's role was filled by the eminent rosarian and plantsman, Graham Stuart Thomas who later became a Consultant. He was succeeded in 1974 by John Sales who is responsible for advising on policy and management for all gardens owned by the Trust.[10]

Purple pansies growing in the bronze vases from La Bagatelle at the Castle's entrance; the colour is echoed by the flowers of Rosmarinus officinalis *beside the arch. (April)*

One of the Gardens Advisers, Jim Marshall, has been directly concerned with Sissinghurst since 1985. The Advisers are called upon to give advice on all matters connected with gardens – technical, managerial, design, historical and botanical, and this is mainly achieved through periodic visits involving discussions with the Head Gardener, Managing Agent and as necessary other regional staff. After each visit the Adviser prepares a detailed report and programme.

The Advisers are also concerned with the conservation and development of plant collections and twenty-six National Collections, such as Colchicums at Felbrigg in Norfolk and pre-1900 shrub roses at Mottisfont Abbey, Hampshire, are held in Trust gardens.

On matters of national importance it is Trust Head Office Committees that are responsible, advised by the Chief Agent and Chief Gardens Adviser. Since 1976 the Gardens Panel, appointed by the Properties Committee, has advised them on policy affecting the acquisition, management and presentation of the Trust's gardens.

The Trust and its gardens thus play a major role in what may be called the thriving garden conservation movement in Britain, and their carefully worked out and experienced philosophy of management and conservation supports our growing national interest in these things. The future of Sissinghurst is in good hands.

THE VIEW
FROM THE TOWER

A tower is the most romantic of buildings and essential to any Sleeping Beauty's castle. The presence of Sissinghurst's tower is all-pervasive in the garden, and it has become the romantic symbol of this place. It is an Elizabethan gatehouse tower of brick, with octagonal turrets and mullioned windows. It is an age-old symbol of home; it can be seen from far away along the road, and from its height, it provides its owner with a warning of approaching friend or foe and a comforting survey of her kingdom. For Vita, the discovery of Sissinghurst's tower was a moment of recognition, for it belongs to the age of chivalry, as she felt she did, and it resembles ancient towers at the Sackville houses of Bolebroke and Old Buckhurst in Sussex. She immortalized her tower in her most pensive poetry: in *Absence*, her sonnet written in 1931 –

Above *Vita's writing-room in the tower.*
Opposite *The view from the tower towards the former farm buildings.*

*No lights are burning in the ivory tower
Like a tall lily in the moonlight risen;*[1]

and in her most romantic novel, *Family History* (1932) when she cast Sissinghurst as the home of her hero, Miles Vane-Merrick: 'The heavy golden sunshine enriched the old brick with a kind of patina, and made the tower cast a long shadow across the grass, like the finger of a gigantic sundial veering slowly with the sun.'[2] She regarded it as her refuge, and claimed it immediately for her own. She established her lair, her writing-room and library, on the first floor above the arch, and also installed the Minerva platen printing press, which she bought from Leonard and Virginia Woolf's Hogarth Press, as she fancied doing what the Woolfs did, a little jobbing printing of her own work. She had electric light installed, and the fireplace made usable, but her room was still usually bitterly cold; she endured it, like many of the other characteristic discomforts of Sissinghurst in winter. She enjoyed it when the wind and snow howled about her tower, and she loved to go up to the tower-roof and watch over her fields, to see the ploughing patterns being made or the firewood being hauled home, and to keep an eagle eye on her gardeners. Her tower was her very private world, in the midst of her garden; in her day no one ventured up the stairs uninvited.

Today, Vita's writing-room is virtually unchanged from the day she left it, in the summer of 1962. Her gardeners keep up the tradition of placing fresh flowers upon her desk and on the tables. Sometimes it seems an unbearable intrusion to gaze upon her private treasures, her books and blue glass, but it is always a pleasure to climb the stairs in anticipation of the view of the garden from the tower roof. The tower is such a magical object in this setting, it gives us wings and takes us half-way to heaven. It encourages a seductive intimacy with the very form and shape of the garden, and yet there is still the fascination of the corners that cannot be seen, of the surprises that have to await investigation on the ground. The Nicolsons first planned their garden from the tower, and this bird's-eye view was of immense assistance to Harold when he was refining the layout. Today the view from the roof reveals all the wit and clarity of his mind and the bones of design that keep the poetic wilderness at bay. All they had had to start with were the walls, and not all of them. This is not a garden made within an old walled garden, as others are, but a garden made within the walls of a vanished house. Modern archaeologists, especially those most interested in gardens, would learn much more than we now know by trial diggings, but it is too late for that. The Nicolsons investigated their ruin fairly thoroughly, and saved all the substantial walls they found: those either side of the tower, with a fragment jutting out at the north end of the tower lawn, and the long wall of the rose garden. Vita felt Sissinghurst's walls were particularly slim and roseate; their slimness is a mark of Tudor building, and may have something to do with Horace Walpole's charge that the Bakers only built for show. Their rosiness, which varies surprisingly in different lights, is also attributed to that peculiar quality of bricks made from clay akin to the soil on which they stand. This is good brickmaking country, even the Romans found it so, and the clay for the Castle's bricks was dug from the hollows that now make the lake, and they were fired in kilns fuelled from Roundshill Wood, beyond the lake. The additions that were made in the thirties, the wall across the north end of the entrance court, and the semi-circular wall that closes the west end of the rose garden, as well as the necessary patching to the old walls, were done with carefully matched bricks. The only other important old bone is the moat wall on the south side of the orchard which was buried in brambles and soil, where centuries of rubbish had been tipped into it. The wall was a precious legacy of grander times, and it can be imagined how the water formerly spread to where the South Cottage stands on higher land.

Convolvulus elegantissimus, which loves a dry, sunny place, flowers at the corner of the tower steps in midsummer. (June)

Left *The view from the tower towards Castle Farmhouse in the distance, the frame yards and kitchen garden; this is the workshop area of the garden behind the rose garden wall. The greenhouses have been built by the National Trust so that as many of Sissinghurst's plants as possible are supplied by in-house propagation. The greenhouses are mildly heated, and with these and the cold frames, the gardeners can keep the majority of the garden's stock going, occasionally buying in trees, roses and bulbs. (May)*

The old walls dictated the form of the garden and inspired the first ideas. Vita had fallen in love with the tower because it could be hers, but at the back of her mind was always the memory of Cardinal Bourchier's tower that overlooked the Green Court at Knole. Her entrance court, like the Green Court, was to be a plain enclosure, a refuge on arrival from the outside world, where the surrounding gables, windows, and chimneys, and the clock and flag on the tower, could shout 'Welcome home'. The awkwardness of its unequal 'rectangle' was cleverly disguised by planting flowers to draw attention to its best features and mask the awkward corners. The closing wall across the north end gave the chance of a large, south facing border, which has always been planted in royal purples, wines and mauves.

Through the Cardinal's tower, Knole has a second court, the Stone Court; through Sissinghurst's tower there would be another court also. Though Vita often longed for a paved one, which she would plant with carpets of tiny flowers, she could never afford the paving, and it was not appropriate. At Knole the Stone Court leads directly into the Great Hall; at Sissinghurst the tower lawn leads out into the wilder garden, the orchard, once the site of the vanished house, but now an essential transition to a greener, softer world. This was the unconscious genesis of the tower lawn; a new enclosing wall would have been totally wrong, a yew hedge was ideal.

After the walls, the secondary bones of Sissinghurst are the hedges. These were not planted to any given style or design, or to make classical garden-rooms; as in other gardens, they were planted in direct response to the needs of this place. The first row of tiny yews, to enclose the tower lawn, were planted in the spring of 1932. That the line of the hedge should spring from a definite point (one side of the gate in the rose garden wall), and that, having sprung, it should continue to another definite point (the northernmost boundary of the garden at the lane beyond the Priest's House) was a logical

Following page *The view from the tower looking south, with the Rondel on the right of the photograph. This view shows how exactly Harold adjusted the classical device of a circle within a square to bring order to Sissinghurst's obtuseness. The gate in the wall from the tower lawn to the old kitchen garden was his starting point, and he designed the hedged circle with a long vista right through to the head of the lime walk. Dark yew hedges make up the Rondel circle, which receives its name and proportions from the hop drying floor of the traditional oasthouses. Lighter hedges of looser texture, in hornbeam, are used to lessen the impact of the lines which are not geometrically correct. The substantial hedge, (originally holly but eventually replanted with yew by the Nicolsons) which divides the rose garden from the cottage garden makes a definite break which modifies the coffin-like shape of the rose garden. The lime walk, with its pleached limes in full leaf, is beyond, and beyond that is the lake field. This side of the old Tudor wall, beneath a 'window' that is marked with an iron grill, was the site of the Lion Pond, Sissinghurst's only formal water. This was abandoned by Vita because the water stagnated; the corner is still damp and shady and grows ferns, mosses, hostas and meconopsis. (October)*

expression of Harold's classical temperament. It is the first mark of his firm designer's hand, guided by, but not enslaved to, a knowledge of architecture which defines the garden. When the second row of yews was planted the following autumn, and the paving was laid between the rows, the yew walk was born. The garden now had two important vistas, through from the entrance, via the tower arch, to the orchard, and – at a sweep – across the garden from north to south from the rose garden to the White Garden.

There was another memory of Knole in the way that the old kitchen garden lay on the south side of the courtyard layout, though Sissinghurst's garden was minute compared to the great garden walled in Kent ragstone at Knole. The Sissinghurst garden does not appear to have been walled, though it was still in cultivation for vegetables when the Nicolsons bought it, and stoutly hedged in thorn to guard it from straying cattle. They decided that this was to be their main flower garden; it was south-facing and conveniently close to the frame yards, the greenhouses and potting sheds, which occupied the space between the Castle and the farmhouse. Their own vegetables could be grown here too, if vegetables and flowers were separated off in some way. Vita's taste in plants allowed for herbs, for fruits (figs and peaches) climbing her garden walls, perhaps for alliums but never coloured cabbages, however curly and decorative. Nor did she share the Jekyll fashion for mixing vegetables with flowers. There was to be a firm divide, and after much discussion they decided on their most expensive wall, which A. R. Powys insisted on building in a semi-circle (and thank goodness he did so) and in which Vita buried a 1935 penny before it was quite finished. The curve, she realized, gave them generous wall space for fruit-growing. The magnificent clematis 'Perle d'Azur' and *Parthenocissus henryana* which now head the rose garden like some rich reredos were planted by the present gardeners.

There were many dreams of Italian gardens in their garden-making, and Sissinghurst's individuality stems from the way those dreams came convoluted from the mind. The hedged-circle in yew, carefully springing from the gateway to the tower lawn, is partly of Italian inspiration. At Vita's insistence its measurement, as its name – the Rondel – reflected the traditional name and shape of Kentish oasthouse floors, where the hops lay in mounds. The paths and beds of the surrounding garden were made by careful centerings and quarterings on the circle, the whole having a perceived balance within its rectangle. The cottage garden, in front of the South Cottage, was simply centred, the crossing aligned to its front door, within its own rough square; separating off the cottage garden alleviated the coffin-shape of the Rondel enclosure. The other cottage, the Priest's House, stood on the northern boundary of the garden, in the corner of a rectangle, now framed by the yew walk and the wall of the tower lawn. This rectangle was given a simple crossing, with a central square. It was first planted with roses, so that their scent could be enjoyed whilst the family ate dinner outside on summer evenings.

The final bone structuring at Sissinghurst was the most brilliant, and appears in no other garden. Somewhere, at the back of his mind, Harold had kept the image of a walk sheltered by pleached limes; I think the image might well have come from the lime walk around the old west garden at Hatfield House, for it was at a ball there, in 1912, that he managed to tell Vita that he loved her. Their first intention was to make a lime walk that surrounded the southern half of their garden, around the rose garden and right along to the moat. When they gave this further thought they realized that the nuttery was in the way; the treasured hazel trees neatly planted in rows, so handy for their nuts but also yielding springy sticks for beans and peas and rose hoops, brought the idea of the lime walk to a stop. Then Harold had hoped to get a continuous vista from the rose garden, through the nuttery to the moat, where he had already planned that a suitably noble statue would survey his handiwork, and be gazed upon in turn. That clearly did not work

either. The compromise was two vistas, the moat walk itself, which was created by masking the difficult bank of the nuttery by covering it with azaleas, and his completely new lime walk, made on the southern border of the garden, with the limes lined up on a row of hazel trees to link everything together. The lime walk, first planted as an avenue of common limes, is now made up of *Tilia platyphyllos 'Rubra'*, trained on horizontal wires, and carefully cut and tied twice a year in the growing season. This is pleaching, a fairly harsh treatment, in the French tradition, as Harold intended, and it requires one of the most skilful of all garden operations. He loved to try it himself, despite Vita's constant worrying that he would fall off the ladder, and that – on his own admission – he was not too good: '. . . when I had finished the lime walk, it looked as if a giraffe had strayed into the garden and taken large munches out of the trees'.[3]

For several years the lime walk was just that, paved in stone, ornamented with oil jars brought home from Italy, and leading directly to the nuttery, where the polyanthus carpet covered the ground in springtime. In the last years before the War Harold became interested in spring flowers, and after the War, in the late forties and early fifties, he perfected his idea of alpine planting.

Once the garden's skeleton was established the Nicolsons planted hedges of plain yew, holly, or hornbeam to extend their old Castle's walls. The simplicity of these hedges is essential to Sissinghurst; they wanted no tapestry effects of mixed plants (though Vita did enjoy the occasional *Tropaeolum speciosum* wreathing through the yew) and no flourishes of topiary. The scale and trimness of the hedges are the most carefully guarded elements of the garden. The Nicolsons had to wait patiently for their hedges to grow, and then they were kept in order by hand cutting with shears, by hands skilled over many years. George Taylor was the gardener with this task in Vita's last years, and up until the mid-seventies; now the hedges are cut by electric shears, except for the box edgings in the White Garden, still trimmed to a string line with hand shears. The yew hedges are cut right back periodically, one side at a time, to allow new growth from their stems, and this tricky operation is now accomplished with practised skill and great success.

Besides the pattern of walls, hedges and paths the view from the tower also reveals the importance of the 'punctuation marks' as designers call them, which were precious to the Nicolsons. The Irish yews which mark the path from the entrance, and the four in the cottage garden, were companions chosen from memories of Long Barn. There they had been amongst Vita's earliest plantings when she began her gardening, placed in a row along her Pleasaunce terrace, in memory of Italian cypresses. The Lombardy poplars also came as memorials to Long Barn, and to French holidays; they are notoriously short-lived and the avenue at the entrance is sadly depleted, but they are being replaced.

Undoubtedly, the most important statue in the garden is Dionysus, who, his arm across his tousled curls, seems to gaze across the orchard and up the moat walk. He watches from either approach, rather like the Mona Lisa. He arrived at Sissinghurst on 20 March 1946, with much concern on Vita's part as to whether the lorry could get right down to the moat. It did. He was voted 'a real triumph', their joint indulgence, paid for between them, 'large as life', a real god to grace their garden and which they had chosen from the dealer Bert Crowther's collection of treasures at Syon Lodge in London. Vita was to become a regular customer of Mr Crowther. It is Dionysus who completes those two important vistas across the garden, his presence arrests the view and his stern gaze commands the paths to be mown across the orchard to please him.

No other statue or ornament exerts quite the imperious control over the garden that Dionysus does, but nothing is in the garden by accident, nor is there any haphazard sprinkling of ornaments. Three sets of magnificent vases decorate the garden, two pairs at the entrance and one pair on the tower steps. These bronze vases came from the garden of

Previous page *Autumn shadows on the orchard, as seen from the tower, in October 1989. The orchard is bounded by the moat, which is in front of the statue of Dionysus on the right, and behind the little white gazebo on the left. Sissinghurst's most venerable trees, which shelter the garden from east winds, are the oaks which line the moat. The orchard is in the process of renewal after the devastation of the great storm of October 1987 which destroyed thirty of its trees. This was one area that the Nicolsons left much as they found, but the mown path on the right illustrates the alignment of Dionysus at the end of the vista from the tower lawn and the break in the yew walk. (October)*

La Bagatelle near Paris, and they had been made specially for the Marquis of Hertford and copied from the Claude Balin originals at Versailles by specific permission from Napoleon III. The Marquis of Hertford bequeathed them to Sir Richard Wallace, and Lady Wallace passed them in turn to Sir John Murray Scott. Sir John had been one of Lady Sackville's most fervent admirers and he gave her almost anything she asked for from the fabulous Wallace Collection, including these vases. She took them to her garden at Knole and finally gave them to Vita for Sissinghurst. The original pots in the lime walk were gigantic jars which Harold ordered before the War from a Venetian potter, for £10. At the same time he bought the pot that is in the centre of the White Garden for £17 in Cairo; he thought it was Egyptian but it is now thought to be Chinese Ming dynasty. The festooned pillar base that sits in the orchard surrounded by *Polygonum affine 'Superbum'* has a long story; it came to Sissinghurst in 1936 after Harold had bought it at a sale because he discovered that it came from Shanganagh Castle in County Dublin, where it was set up by a Nicolson ancestor to commemorate the Reform Bill of 1832. Apparently six years later, in disillusionment, the same ancestor added the inscription *Alas to this date a humbug.*

The view from the tower also reveals the small army of old sinks ranged along the opposite wall of the entrance court. Many of these were unearthed from the rubbish of

Opposite *The entrance courtyard, from beside the library door, on a wet April morning showing the chaenomeles – which Vita knew as* Cydonia japonica *and which tones so well with the bricks. Purple auriculas are just coming into flower in the terracotta pots. The texture lines of the lawn and the tightly wired Irish yews are a present-day image of good garden management, but friends of Vita's remember how she loved 'enammel'd daisy carpets' and her yews left shaggy. Neither daisies nor shaggy yews are healthy in long-term management practice, but it is worth asking if conservation should not seek a compromise between the romantic tastes of the garden-maker and the horticultural excellence of modern professionals. (April)*

Left *The pale yellowy-green racemes of* Ribes laurifolium, *an evergreen currant, provide early flowering interest in March.*

Below Osteospermum ecklonis prostratum, *a tangle of aromatic leaves with daisy-like flowers which open in the sun – but remain closed on dull days – fills one of the sinks against the wall of the entrance court. The purply touches of these flowers tone beautifully with those of the long-spurred hybrid aquilegia and the* Solanum crispum *'Glasnevin' in full flower. (April)*

Sissinghurst, and eagerly commandeered by Vita as homes for plants. She loved alpine flowers, again because of holiday memories – flower hunting and walking expeditions above Val d'Isère – and frequently came home with a burst of enthusiasm for making small gardens or planting alpines between pavings and stones. One of her first, very amateurish, garden ideas was for a sink which would contain three kinds of saxifrage, two kinds of dianthus, an iris, thyme, soldanella and campanula. By the time she came to Sissinghurst she had settled for spikes of tiny iris, alliums or grape hyacinths growing with carpets of thyme or saxifrage; she filled a whole sink with *Omphalodes verna* with its forget-me-not flowers on a rich green covering of leaves. She was always very conscious that some people had to do their gardening in tiny spaces, in window-boxes or small troughs, and she would actually make-up offerings of collected winter treasures in beds of moss for house-bound friends. This concern with the minutiae of gardening was an unusual paradox, the very opposite of her 'squirishness' and love of bushes of effusive roses, and was just another aspect of her complex personality expressed in her garden.

Some of the earliest plantings at Sissinghurst are in the courtyard, around its walls and on those facing the tower lawn. The rose 'Allen Chandler', a crimson-scarlet climber which Hugh Dickson introduced in 1924, was planted each side of the entrance arch, and flowers there still. On the outside of the entrance, echoed at the foot of the tower, are the

Right *The length of the purple border viewed from outside the library door in August. Here are large clumps of* Eryngium × tripartitum, *a prickly mass of metallic mauve, purple* Salvia × superba, *pink dianthus and pink verbena, a deep pink Michaelmas daisy, purple petunias and magenta dahlias. Also in the foreground are the leaves of the small Iris 'Sissinghurst'.*

Above *The purple border looking west, towards the library door. The shapely heps of* Rosa moyesii *dominate the sweep of the autumn border, in which dahlias, Michaelmas daisies and eryngiums keep up the colourful effect. (September)*

enormous clumps of rosemary, which often left barely a pathway in Vita's day and offered their scented leaves to be brushed by passing hands. Now the classic *Rosmarinus officinalis* has been joined by the finer feathers of *R.* 'Sissinghurst'. The much-loved *Rosa wichuraiana* rambler, 'Albertine', climbs the tower, its copper-coloured buds and salmon-pink flowers toning perfectly with the bricks. Other traditional inhabitants of the courtyard are an orangey-scarlet flowered Chaenomeles, *Solanum crispum* 'Glasnevin', *Ceanothus* 'Southmead' and an enormous *Hydrangea petiolaris* wreathed over the gate leading into the rose garden. At the opposite end of the courtyard is the regal splash of purples, reds and mauves called the purple border, a deeper echo of the spectrum of colours that traditionally belongs in the rose garden. This border reflects how well the Victorian shade of magenta has been strained into twentieth-century flowers, but it is still a difficult colour to handle. The purple border represents Vita's independence of the restraints Gertrude Jekyll imposed upon gardeners, which will be further explored. Here are all the crimson reds and royal purples that Miss Jekyll suggested were difficult. She tackled them via her rhododendrons, placing what she called the cool, clear purples of the *ponticum* varieties in the shade, on their own, or with white flowers. The crimsons and blood reds and claret colours were to be elsewhere, in the sun. In perennial plantings Miss Jekyll only used a little of any of these colours, as the peak of colour intensity in the border. Vita though, characteristically, threw the complete range into one, sun-drenched setting; she loved the darkened burgundies and maroons of Renaissance paintings and the crimsons and scarlets of the warm south, and this collection of flowers brings a fiery glow to cool, temperate England. The purples begin with wallflowers, tulips, pansies and *Iris* 'Sissinghurst', and hardy geraniums, columbines, *Campanula glomerata* and the scarlet flowers of *Rosa moyesii* follow. The border seems to intensify in colour as summer progresses, especially if the weather is hot. There is reason enough for royal adjectives – panoplies and processions of dark purple delphiniums, bergamot, *Liatris spicata*, clematis, penstemons and dahlias with Michaelmas daisies, fuchsias – and as crowning glory, the scarlet heps of *Rosa moyesii* against the varying burgundies of the vine leaves on the wall.

Sissinghurst's purple border, viewed from the tower, resembles a rich tapestry, draped from the wall to the ground. In recent years purple plants have become extremely popular, especially red and purple leaved shrubs and perennials, which prolong the season of colour to the much-vaunted 'all year round'. Sissinghurst is not a place for slick carpets or swathes of such dull inventions, which Vita would have despised.

It is perhaps worthwhile, with this view from the tower, to try and establish just what this garden is, and what it is not. It is a rare and unusual garden, made predominantly in two periods, the 1930s and the 1940s/50s to the particular tastes of two people, neither of whom could be called followers of fashion. They had their own tastes and were satisfied with them; when Vita refuted the help of professionals at Sissinghurst she should perhaps have made allowance for A. R. Powys' heart searchings and for much advice, freely given, by her friends Edward Ashdown Bunyard, Colonel Hoare Grey, 'Cherry' Collingwood Ingram, James Russell and Hilda Murrell, but in essence she was speaking the truth. The Nicolsons listened to their advisers, but then took their own decisions; they were trend-setters of great independence. The bones of Sissinghurst were achieved by Harold (after much argument with Vita who conceived affections for various old plants which were always in the way of his vistas) by cool exercise of his classical judgement, by fulfilling expectations and creating order. Sissinghurst's sequence of

The centre of the purple border in the courtyard. This colourful flowering is made up of lavender and magenta dahlias, a rich wine red bergamot, purple spikes of Liatris spicata, a single dark purple delphinium and masses of pink, purple and mauve clematis. (July)

Above *Courtyard façade of the entrance arch. The red roses in flower are the famous climber 'Allen Chandler' and the pink flowers belong to the noisette climber with tea scented flowers, first bred in the mid nineteenth-century, 'Gloire de Dijon'. (May)*

Below *A pretty harbinger of autumn at the foot of the walls of Nigel Nicolson's house in the courtyard,* Nerine bowdenii *'Praecox'. (October)*

galleries and rooms, it is worth repeating, grew naturally from his organization of the ruins of the Bakers' original house. He was doing the exact opposite to what Major Lawrence Johnston had done at Hidcote Manor, which was to fling brave vistas out into empty fields, and then attach garden-rooms to them.

The design of Sissinghurst is the product of a sensitive understanding of the place, of masking its bad features, such as those coffin-shaped spaces, and enhancing its virtues. It is just this flowering of its 'sense of place' that makes it such a satisfying garden; it is completely true to itself. But, in the train of Edwin Lutyens's magnificently architectural gardens constructed like houses out-of-doors, and an early twentieth-century rediscovery of the gardens of Italian Renaissance villas, gardens made up of outdoor rooms were designated *the* twentieth-century style. Old walled gardens were revived and country house architects who remained loyally classical in the face of the Modern Movement, designed sequential spaces around restored eighteenth-century houses or their classical revivals. A garden-room can be a ballroom or a tiny den in scale, and flexibility is just what the modern garden lover requires: so many people have found in Sissinghurst's rooms the dream and the reality of gardens they could make for themselves, that it is easy to forget how highly individual the original is.

Along with the plethora of imitations of the English classical revival style come a whole host of familiar furnishings, which it is well to note that Sissinghurst does *not* have: it has no long grass-walk flanked by double borders, no pergola, no pools or fountains, no trellis walks or arbours and no topiary twists or triangles. There are no white painted seats, no Versailles tubs, there is no iris rill nor laburnum tunnel, no balustraded terrace or columned temple, and there are very definitely no Japanese touches or *trompe l'oeil* effects. There are plenty of such things in other gardens. Here most of them would have been dismissed with a snort, and the Sackville insult – *bedint*– meaning common.

The last view from the tower is the unfolding of the garden into the fields of Castle Farm and beyond into the farmed landscape of Kent. This is the Weald of Kent, the heart of the 'Garden of England', so long worked by man that it is almost 'gardenesque', a neat coloured landscape ornamented by the most wonderful collection of picturesque villages, of white clad windmills and white topped oasthouses, of crooked and leaning half-timbered cottages, and clusterings of dun and rust coloured farmsteads; the old bricks of Sissinghurst have plenty of company. There are still orchards and hop gardens but much fewer than there used to be; apples, cherries and hops seem no longer major economical factors in local life, but more a part of local tradition clung to for tradition's sake and cash sales at the farm gate.

In 1930 the Nicolsons bought Sissinghurst because they could be in the heart of the country and within easy reach of London, and since then thousands have followed in their wake; Sissinghurst sits amidst smart commuter countryside, a restored jewel among little jewels of restoration by people with a fashionable taste for traditional interiors. Its countryside is abundant in bed and breakfasts, and the heritage industry is rapidly growing. Although just excluded from the Area of Outstanding Natural Beauty, Sissinghurst nestles in a tourist landscape within easy reach of mighty Canterbury or still spa-like Tunbridge Wells, taking in the National Trust's picturesque Scotney, an old castle which no one wanted to *live* in but made a garden around, the Lamberhurst vineyards, Finchcocks Musical Instrument Museum and Forstal Farm Craft Centre. In terms of literary landscape it lies half way between Chaucer's Pilgrim's Way and Henry James's Rye – half way perhaps in more than geographical terms. Politically, this is traditionally Tory ground; in horticultural values Sissinghurst lies between Bedgebury National Pinetum, a fascinating and beautiful collection of conifers, eight miles to the south-west, which is the best in Europe, and the gardeners' paradise of Great Dixter at

Northiam, ten miles due south, owned by the writer and gardener Christopher Lloyd. The Pinetum is on the edge of the old Bedgebury Forest, a reminder that this was once the wooded countryside of wealden iron smelting and charcoal burners, and that Sissinghurst forms part of a cluster of *hursts* or wooded places – Lamberhurst, Goudhurst, Hawkhurst and Staplehurst. In some views of this countryside the once great wealden forest of Anderida seems not too far from the imagination. But Sissinghurst has always been on the highroad to Europe and this has had a considerable influence on its fate: the Norman invasion introduced the de Saxinherstes and de Berhams into its story, in the sixteenth century it hosted Queen Elizabeth I on her way to Dover, and in 1952 Harold was encouraged to make the White Garden to please the European visitors who stopped en route to the Festival of Britain. It is interesting to speculate what effect the opening of the Channel Tunnel will have when our days as an island race are ended and the highway will carry even more potential visitors past the signposts to Sissinghurst.

The view from the tower of the White Garden in May, with the magnolia trees in flower. It is this chance of a bird's-eye view which adds to the magical effect of Sissinghurst, and here, in the White Garden before the plants take over, the crisp outlines of its bone structure stand out like a child's model garden. It can be clearly seen that the first, or southern, half of the garden is made up of four large beds, which are guarded by the little statue of the Vestal Virgin, who stands on the left. The iron frame holding the burgeoning canopy of Rosa mulliganii is the centrepoint of the plan, and beyond this are the complex quartered beds edged in box which each hold a different kind of white flower.

THE ROSE GARDEN

From the very beginning the Nicolsons intended that Sissinghurst should be a garden filled with roses. Roses were to be planted to climb over the old trees in the orchard, and to fill beds in the Priest's House garden and the old kitchen garden. The Priest's House garden had been laid out, quartered around a central square, by the summer of 1932; the old kitchen garden required rather more thought and persuasion. On one lovely dry and warm morning in March 1932 Harold wrote in his diary of their first attempts – 'Viti and I measure the kitchen garden to discover how much paling will be required to make it square. I fiddle about with this vista problem. Obviously what would be good in a teleological sense would be to put the end of the main nuttery walk at the end of a main vista running from the new angle of the kitchen garden, past the cottage garden and thus

Above *Vista through the Rondel. (May)*
Opposite *The long south facing border of the rose garden. (June)*

Above *On the south side of the gateway through to the tower lawn the rose 'Frühlingsgold' flowers against the hazy purple and green backdrop of* Clematis macropetala. *(May)*

Opposite *A close-up of 'Madame Lauriol de Barny' with her pink blossoms interspersed with deep blue aquilegias and on the right a blue ceanothus, in typical Sissinghurst style. (June)*

Below *'Souvenir du Docteur Jamain', the old French hybrid perpetual rose which dates from 1860, has a very special place at Sissinghurst; Vita found it blooming, unregarded, in an old nursery and brought it home and grew it on. When it was subsequently identified as this wonderful crimson-maroon velvet rose she could rightly claim to have returned it to our gardens. (June)*

perspectively to what is now a gate into a field, but which one day will be a classic statue erect among cherry trees. Only this cuts angularly across the holly hedge in our own little cottage garden, and fits in obtusely with the rest of the design. That is what is such a bore about Sissinghurst. It is magnificent but constantly obtuse ... disturbed by these considerations we weed the delphinium bed ...'.[1]

Before long they tried again, having had the idea of an enormous circle in the centre of the shape that resisted becoming a square, and this successfully gave the impression of flower beds quartered around a centre in traditional fashion. The hedged yew circle, the Rondel as it was called, took time to grow, but within ten years the beds of the obtuse garden were famous for their roses. So much so that *Country Life* asked Vita to write about them, which she did for the issue of 11 September 1942. 'Visitors who look for the hybrid teas and perpetuals will be disappointed,' she began. 'For one thing the soil is too light to suit them, and for another they have not particularly interested the owners. The speciality, if it may so pretentiously be named, lies in the collection of musk and old fashionable-roses, neither rare in themselves nor difficult to obtain, but perhaps not often seen growing in profusion.'[2]

It would be a mistake to assume that the present-day battle of tastes between Hybrid Tea fans and old rose lovers began here, at Sissinghurst! The Nicolsons had grown a lot of Hybrid Teas in the rich clay soil at Long Barn – the coppery 'Betty', apricot 'Lady Hillingdon', the pinks 'Killarney' and 'Lady Ashtown'. They genuinely felt that the old shrub roses gave them more in return for a given amount of labour and expense. The key word was the last one, 'profusion' – they loved the generosity of spirit of a plant that flowers with gusto, that gives its all with great fountains of scented colour for a glorious performance in June. They felt that Sissinghurst 'lent itself kindly to their untidy, lavish habit; there was space in plenty, with the walls to frame their exuberance, and consequently they may be found foaming in an unorthodox way in the midst of flower borders ...'.[3] The rose garden, as it was photographed for *Country Life* in the last season before wartime neglect took a toll on its beauty, was filled with Damask, cabbage, Gallica and Hybrid Musk roses. The Hybrid Musk roses, the Rev. Joseph Pemberton's hybrids 'no less lovely than their names' were ranged down the long border in front of the wall – the yellow 'Danaë', 'Penelope's' glossy foliage and creamy pink flowers, 'Felicia', so strongly aromatic with pink flowers, the smaller shrub 'Thisbe' with yellow flowers, 'Pax' with large creamy flowers, and the most famous of all 'Moonlight' with its truly musky fragrance and foaming creamy flowers on dark stems. Their scent, wrote Vita, was 'almost too strong on a summer evening'.

The collection of Pemberton hybrids was prominent amongst the roses of Sissinghurst, and their exuberant flowering in the rose garden was the first sight for which Sissinghurst became known. The Nicolsons were fairly content to allow the garden its glorious performance in midsummer, and not ask Nature for more. The Gallicas and cabbage roses (Centifolias), all grown to great size and unclipped freedom, were ranged in the other beds. They were chosen for their scent and lovely flowers, but also for their names, historic and poetic, and the dreams they could inspire, which Vita poured into her poems. The Gallicas included that most romantic of all roses, Rosa Mundi, striped and named for 'Fair Rosamunde', the dark purple 'Cardinal de Richelieu', the Old Velvet rose called 'Tuscany' and two crimsons 'Alain Blanchard' and 'Charles de Mills'. Amongst the collection of Centifolias were 'Tour de Malakoff' (for which David Austin's description is irresistible – 'A rich, sumptuous beauty, with large open flowers ... at first magenta-purple, turning to rich parma violet and later to lavender and grey'[4].) Also there were 'Chapeau de Napoléon' (R. × *centifolia* 'Cristata') with its 'mossy' buds and pink flowers and the famous blush pink named after the painter,

The north-west corner of the rose garden in midsummer.
In the foreground is the Pemberton hybrid musk 'Vanity'
which has a sweet-pea scent, and beyond it are large
clumps of Alchemilla mollis *and* Salvia × superba.
The walls are covered with the rich greenery of
Hydrangea petiolaris, *on the right, and a fig tree in the*
corner beside the archway. (June)

'Fantin–Latour'. Vita proudly claimed to have revived another of her favourite roses, the Victorian Hybrid Perpetual 'Souvenir du Docteur Jamain'. She wrote, 'I found him growing against the office wall of an old nursery. No one knew what he was; no one seemed to care; no one knew his name; no one had troubled to propagate him. Could I dig him up, I asked? Well, if you like to risk it, they said, shrugging their shoulders; it's a very old plant, with a woody stiff root. I risked it; 'Docteur Jamain' survived his removal; and now has a flourishing progeny in my garden and also on the market of certain rosarians to whom I gave him. 'Docteur Jamain' is a deep red, not very large flowers [sic], but so sweetly and sentimentally scented. Some writers would call it nostalgically scented, meaning everything that burying one's nose into the heart of a rose meant in one's childhood, or in one's adolescence when one first discovered poetry, or the first time one fell in love'. Typically she finishes on a practical note, this rose not liking too much sun . . . 'he burns. A South-west aspect suits him better than full south'.[5]

When she wrote about her old roses in this way it did a great deal for their revival; now that they have flooded back into favour and into our gardens it is easy for us to understand her passion, and the way in which they appeared to her almost as personalities. But it was new then. 'Who was Charles de Mills? Who was Madame

Hardy?' she asked: 'I wish I could find out who Madame Lauriol (de Barny) was in real life, to have so sumptuous a flower called after her. I suspect that she may have belonged to the *haute cocotterie* of Paris . . . or possibly I misjudge her and she may have been the perfectly respectable wife of some M. de Barny, perhaps a rose-grower at Lyons . . .'.[6] She wishes someone would write biographies of roses, and of course though this has been pursued a little way, there are so many mysteries still.

It is easy to see how Vita's poetic mind became obsessed with such magnificent flowers which bore these intriguing names; the Rondel roses were collected with an intellectual relish. They not only filled the garden with their colours and scented presence, but they also brought with them the romance of classical history, the richness of Renaissance Italy, and not a little of poor, godless Vita's awe of the majesty of the Roman liturgy, of which she wrote at length in *The Garden*, – of 'other blood-red points where I had been . . .'

> *St Mark's in Venice on an Easter-day*
> *Deep as the petals of Arabian rose,*
> *When a great Cardinal in robes arose*
> *Tremendous in the pulpit . . . .*[7]

This is what her roses meant to her. It was good to surmise, and to make the most of her memories through them. The precious pink Damask rose 'Ispahan' was collected along with many other plants vaguely Persian, for the sake of the Nicolsons' shared passion for that country. Harold had been posted to Teheran in the mid-twenties and was the first to be captivated. Vita soon visited him, on two celebrated trips in 1926 and 1927 which she described in *Passenger to Teheran* and *Twelve Days*, her two highly-praised books of travel writing. She was completely overwhelmed by the beauty and mystery of the desert and the timeless traditions of a way of life so ancient that even her beloved Knole and nearly four hundred years of Sackvilles seemed but a moment. They tramped

The dais within the curved wall at the west end of the rose garden is the setting for the large, wave-backed seat designed by Edwin Lutyens, flanked by two lead vases. The plants that curtain the wall, here in their autumn guise, are Clematis *'Perle d'Azur' interwreathed with the vine,* Parthenocissus henryana, *and the crimson-leaved* Vitis vinifera. *The seat, along with the smaller one at the end of the long border, also a design by Lutyens, came to Sissinghurst via Vita's mother, Lady Sackville. Lutyens designed three gardens for her in London and Brighton, and gave her the seats, which were originally made for other gardens. Though Lutyens helped the Nicolsons with their garden at Long Barn, he never came to Sissinghurst; he is appropriately remembered here for the great influence he had on Harold's design skills. (October)*

the foothills of the Elburz looking for wild flowers and abandoned gardens, and they brought home *Iris persica*, *Anemone x.fulgens*, a small pink gladiolus, some colchicums, *Tulipa sylvestris* and *Tulipa aucheriana* 'like an old and rich brocade'. She fell in love with the city of Isfahan and with many old gardens, and almost any plant with Persian connections – but especially the Persian yellow *Rosa foetida persiana* and the *Rosa foetida* derived 'Star of Persia', were affectionately gathered into her gardens at Long Barn and then here at Sissinghurst.

These were just some of the glorious company of the rose garden in its first flowerings before the War; bare rose beds were not Sissinghurst's style. The edges of the grass paths were crowded with irises of all kinds and, stachys, pinks, alliums and verbascums. Colouring was of the utmost importance, with the dominance of the rich burgundies, crimsons, maroons, magentas, pinks and creamy roses, set off with the slightest touches of yellow and massings of silver-leaved carpets. Every summer Vita became more passionate about her roses, and more knowledgeable; there were many visitors to the rose collection to share her enthusiasms, most notably Edward Ashdown Bunyard, who lived near Maidstone (his father's nursery at Allington raised the famous apple 'Allington Pippin', amongst others) and whose book *Old Garden Roses* was published in 1936. Sadly Bunyard died three years later, leaving the old rose revival largely in the capable hands of Graham Stuart Thomas. After the War Graham Thomas' growing collection of old roses at James Russell's Sunningdale Nursery became well-known; when Vita began to write for the *Observer* in 1946, she naturally wrote many pieces on her roses and gave the names of her suppliers – Sunningdale, Murrell's of Shrewsbury, Hillings at Chobham, and smaller nurseries: Daisy Hill at Newry, Co. Down and Archer & Daughter at Sellinge near Ashford.[8]

I have meant to give the impression that the rose garden was far more than a collection of roses and sympathetic flowers; it was really more of an autobiography in plants. For many people who loved Vita it is still a very special, almost hallowed place; certainly it was her first love amongst Sissinghurst's gardens. Somehow the mixing of the memories, and the larger-than-life abundance of the roses were the true expression of her personality.

Vita was rather an expert on old roses long before she began to write her *Observer* pieces and was instrumental in setting the old rose revival on its way – as usual, in the vanguard of fashion. She was, so to speak, a contemporary of the Rev. Pemberton's hybrid musks, which came onto the market during the First War and in the twenties, the years when Vita was avidly learning her gardening by much nursery visiting and catalogue searching. Her rose garden most certainly celebrated the existence of roses as garden beauties, for their form, foliage, flowers, scent and autumn heps; Vita was perfectly capable of assessing this matter for herself, but I think it is fair to say, in the search for her beginnings as a rose expert, that this is the one instance in her gardening where she took notice of Gertrude Jekyll. Miss Jekyll's influence does not appear anywhere else at Sissinghurst; in fact, Vita independently flouted her colour dictums, by favouring a cool and warm mix of blues and oranges (which was her passion at Long Barn), by using – emphasizing – all these purples and magentas which Miss Jekyll said should be treated with great restraint, and by conceiving of a white garden, the single colour Miss Jekyll did not consider, because in her painterly tradition white was the colour that lit all others. However, in the rose garden, Gertrude Jekyll's influence may be given a little credit, and the great gardener enters the Sissinghurst story via her one time protegé, Edwin Lutyens, when, in the summer of 1916, he met Vita's mother, Lady Sackville, and fell in love with her. He eventually took on the role of her devoted lover; he was not rich and could not give her fabulous presents, but he did indulge her patiently with his time, helping her to buy and alter a series of houses and gardens. In August 1917,

The old Hybrid Perpetual rose 'Ulrich Brunner Fils' trained on hazel 'benders' in the rose beds; the colour of the flowers is most deliciously described as 'vivid cerise with a cherry flush'. (June)

eight months after the birth of her son, Nigel, Vita was taken on an outing by her mother, to Munstead Wood in Surrey, to meet, and be approved by, Lutyens's patroness and partner in garden making, Gertrude Jekyll, his 'Aunt Bumps'. It was not an auspicious visit; Vita thought the great gardener 'rather fat and rather grumbly' and the garden not at its best, though 'one can see it must be lovely'. However, she did go home to Long Barn, armed with a very Jekyllian taste in roses, for it was all the Jekyll favourites that she listed in her garden notebook. She never saw Miss Jekyll again, but Lady Sackville and Edwin Lutyens came to spend a weekend at Long Barn in the summer of 1925, when Lutyens helped Harold design a formal garden of brick raised-beds for the lowest part of the garden. By the time they bought Sissinghurst Lutyens's affair with Lady Sackville was fading, and he never came to the Castle. The two seats designed by him are here in the rose garden, one eight feet long and wavy backed, and the smaller seat with two 'nicks' in the back band, originally came from Lady Sackville's garden in Brighton after her death in 1936. They have since been renewed by copying the original designs.

After the Second War the aspect of the rose garden had changed; the Rondel hedges were grown to a full, dark circle and dominated the garden, and the roses and other plants suffered from neglect. All the beds were cleaned and replanted by Jack Vass and his gardeners in the years 1946–8. The species roses which were grown in the Priest's House garden, *Rosa rugosa* '*Alba*', *R. glauca* (syn. *R. rubrifolia*), *R. villosa*, and the one named for Rev. Wolley-Dod, were amongst newcomers, when the decision to make the White

Above *The Rondel photographed by Edwin Smith in the 1960s. The main flowering of the roses is yet to come and the statuesque eremurus bloom against the dark yew hedges. The old wall is wreathed in varieties of clematis, which also do so well at Sissinghurst. A recent count has revealed more than eighty-five varieties in the garden. Here the hedges are the way they were in Vita's lifetime, when they were cut by hand and their bulk was larger.*

Below *Rosa rugosa 'Alba' with mid-August flowers and large orangey heps. (August)*

Garden was made. Vass persuaded Vita that some of the roses should be trained over hazel hoops, an idea he had learned from his former place, Cliveden in Buckinghamshire. The rose garden hedges now made large shady areas where Harold wanted to see pale flowers, tall and waving against the dark yew. It was not so much that the roses changed significantly, but the carpet around and beneath them became richer and more varied.

For pale wands waving against the yew they used rather rare eremuri, tall delicate spikes of the palest pink *Eremurus* Himrob, the white *Eremurus Himalaicus* or yellow E. *Stenophyllus* (syn E. *Bungei*), and added equally pale peonies. Then Harold had a moment of inspiration at a Chelsea Flower Show and became keen to add all kinds of lilies, particularly *L. regale* and *L. auratum*. Certainly in black-and-white photographs taken in the fifties the dark Rondel is surrounded in pale fronds to produce an almost theatrical touch which must have drawn gasps of pleasure. I am not at all sure that some of the credit ought not to go to Constance Spry, who was a frequent visitor to Sissinghurst, and who had written about such effects in her book *Flowers for House and Garden* before the War.[9] She had the same taste in roses, and same rose suppliers as Vita, and they shared an admiration for Norah Lindsay's garden at the Manor House, Sutton Courtenay in Oxfordshire; it is almost impossible – and rarely a useful exercise – to apportion too particular a credit for gardening tastes and ideas, for the best gardeners are usually the strongest individuals, brave enough to do what they want. That certainly applied to all three ladies, Mrs Lindsay, Mrs Spry and Vita, and each had an exquisite taste, and mutual respect for one another. This is worth bearing in mind when trying to build up a picture of how that taste was expressed in ephemeral flowers.

The other luminous spires that found their way into the rose garden included verbascums, foxgloves, hollyhocks, thistly things and the bugbane, *Cimicifuga racemosa*, which produces tall feathery spikes of white flowers in shady conditions in later summer. The smaller mulleins of the Cotswold varieties, 'Cotswold Beauty' or 'Cotswold Queen' ('dusty, fusty, musty in colouring' wrote Vita), four-feet high with spikes of creamy or buff flowers, looked well with 'Tuscany or the old Red Damask or the purple Moss'.[10] Discovery of the giant *Verbascum bombyciferun* (syn. *V.* 'Broussa'), six-foot high, which was planted against the Rondel yews brought lots of comment – 'some strange submarine growth, waving about . . . they ought to be growing in a primeval landscape with a pterodactyl browsing amongst them'. Vita felt they were like Roman candles, and they had the art of arranging themselves into grand, upward curves, which supplied the required effect. In addition there were giant *Onopordum nervosum* (syn. *O. arabicum*), spectacularly thistle-like and steely pale against the yew, and dangerously spiky on close aquaintance. Slightly less prickly were the Eryngiums, especially *E. giganteum*, 'Miss Willmott's Ghost' which has always been grown here. The spires that were missing were lupins, not favoured because they were too solid in colour, and delphiniums, which were a Sissinghurst favourite, but grown elsewhere, near the Priest's House, so that the aspiring tower could be viewed through their blue and silver spikes. There was, it must be admitted, a touch of snobbery here – everyone knew that delphiniums were aristocrats of flowers – but lupins were perhaps too easy, too showy and too coarse; that is how gardeners' tastes are formed

As a companion to the roses, the most familiar flower of the rose garden is the iris – irises pressing against the edges of the stone path, irises beautifully contrasted with great clumps of columbines, iris leaf spikes vying with spikes of stachys and sprouting from clumps of velvety leaves or mounds of *Geranium endressii*. Bearded irises were rather in a decline after the War, and their cultivation at Sissinghurst, which coincided with the appearance of Sir Cedric Morris's wonderful Benton End hybrids, did a great deal for their revival. Irises were happy with the roses – their rhizomes could lie basking in the

sun, unentangled with rose roots, happily accommodating sprinklings of aquilegias. The colours too, were right for the rose garden setting – from the more common purples, which were bred into delicate mauves and lavenders, to the creamy yellows and golds with velvety purple falls. And there were also clumps of the luminous striped leaves of *Iris pallida* 'Variegata', and the small, rosy-purple *Iris graminea*. The iris-like *Sisyrinchium*, with spikes of small yellow flowers, was also planted here.

After the War the Nicolsons tried hard to resist bringing modern, labour-saving ideas into the most precious parts of their garden, and the rose garden was particularly well guarded in this respect. 'Ground covers' was a term brought to gardens from landscape architecture, implying large, boring blankets of something that kept the weeds down. They were not Sissinghurst style. But the spikes and spires of the rose garden were softened by clumps and carpets of delicate, old-fashioned clove pinks and carnations; dear 'Mrs Sinkins', the most familiar of white dianthus, was allowed almost anywhere she chose, and so were the beloved Cheddar pinks. Old World garden pinks of cerise, salmon and pinky shades, and hardy carnations, such as cerise and grey striped 'Harmony' and large flowered 'Lavender Clove' were brought home from the Royal Horticultural Society shows as suitable rose garden residents. Not to be forgotten were mounds of pansies, predominantly with purple and maroon faces, and rather larger clumps of *Sedum* 'Autumn Joy', which was then a rarity as a garden sight. Such tastes caused Harold to be quoted as saying that Vita only liked 'brown' flowers – she certainly

The Medjez-el-Bab gate between the entrance court and the rose garden – a view that explains the reason why the colours of the purple border on the far side of the court reflect those of the rose garden. Verbena 'Sissinghurst' flowers on the right corner of the path. (August)

did have an eye for the darker shades that the nurseryman strove for, but which looked so well with the rich pinks, golds, creams, salmons and mauves that the rose garden displayed.

The second wave of roses enhanced the colour rules: most noticeable were the darkest crimson blooms of 'William Lobb', the shaggy carmine flowers of the French Bourbon 'Madame Isaac Pereire', the leggy Hybrid Perpetual 'Ulrich Brunner Fils' (which was trained on hoops), the dainty pink rose *R.* alba 'Céleste'. A special favourite was the 'most swagger boastful bush' of reddish purple 'ZigeunerKnabe' (sometimes known as 'Gypsy Boy'), which were accompanied by the French aristocrats 'Commandant Beaurepaire', his pink uniform splashed with purple, and the pinks 'Souvenir de la Malmaison' and 'Madame Pierre Oger'.

The shrub companions for this rich company were grown up the rose garden walls, and included collections of ceanothus and clematis. The ceanothus, *C. impressus* and *C. dentatus*, both with very deep blue flowers, the former of rather tighter, smaller foliage, were tender Californian evergreen varieties. The clematis, providing so many wonderfully purply, pinky colourings for the rose garden, included the now-famous *C.* 'Nelly Moser', the purple *C.* 'Gipsy Queen' and the late-flowering Viticella clematis 'Kermesina,' of a deep burgundy colour which Vita particularly liked. 'Kermesina' suited 'to perfection' the other later companions of the rose garden, the Japanese anemones in their pinky and mauve colourings (white are for the White Garden) particularly the deep mauve-pink 'Prinz Heinrich'.

Other later flowers were *Hydrangea aspera villosa*, a lavender lace-cap flower (mophead hydrangeas were specifically banned) which looked good with a clump of *Acanthus spinosus*, and hibiscus with red or lavender flowers, the deep blue plumbago, *Ceratostigma Willmottianum*, and the accommodating lavenders, of which the rose garden sported several varieties, including 'Hidcote' and 'Twickel Purple'.

Under the National Trust's ownership in the late sixties it immediately became clear that the rose garden's narrow grass-paths, soft bands of green between the richly coloured rose beds, would have to be relaid as hard surfaces. The Trust profoundly believed that its property must look its best for visitors at all times; roped-off areas of bare mud or reseeded grass looked both inefficient and inhospitable. The side-paths were laid in pink and dark blue bricks, concreted in, and the long stone paved path in front of the south-facing herbaceous border was relaid on a proper foundation. Vita had loved thymes and sages running through the cracks of this paving, but that is something that is out of the question for a public garden, for the plants are more usually dead than alive. Undoubtedly this work, completed by 1972, changed the character of the rose garden, but it made it more readily enjoyed by more people. The hard edges to the paths have been softened by skilful plantings that grow over the bricks – with large clumps of hardy geraniums, *Alchemilla mollis*, hostas, pulmonaria and the fluffy-headed grasses, the pennisetums. The garden is now perhaps less dominated by roses than it was in Vita's day, partly because old roses are no longer a novelty, (they are in so many gardens and we expect to see them with a certain mix of accompanying plants) and partly because shrubs and herbaceous plants are needed to prolong the season of colour in this, the grandest of Sissinghurst's garden-rooms.

Perhaps the importance of Vita – not as a serious academic researcher, propagator and supplier, but as a romantic, impassioned and indulgent grower of old roses – has yet to be appreciated. It takes all kinds of people to create a revival, and I think it a likely assumption that more gardeners took to hunting for old roses in nurseries because of Vita's inspiration rather than being sent by any of the great books on the subject. There are less old photographs of the rose garden in flower than of other parts of the garden,

The long south facing border of the rose garden in early spring; this photograph makes an interesting comparison with that on page 67 of the same view in full flowering. This was the border that Vita allowed to become the nearest to an herbaceous border in her garden; she considered the Jekyll-style herbaceous border as too labour-intensive and too garish in high summer, so she made a mixed border here, in advance of our idea of such things today. But a mixed border in her terms was still far from the all-year-round colour and foliage that is to a more modern taste, and here the plants are still either underground or showing bare twigs only. The exception is the gigantic Euphorbia characias wulfenii *'Lambrook Gold'; this was named for Mrs Margery Fish's garden at Lambrook Manor in Somerset where it was grown and introduced to gardeners after the War. (March)*

Left *The north west corner of the rose garden, with the path which leads to the door into the frame yards. This is high summer and the colour is kept in the garden with a large* Hydrangea aspera villosa *in full bloom, and mallows, verbena, Michaelmas daisies and clematis. In the foreground the iris leaves, with the variegated* Iris pallida *on the right, crowd to the edge of the path as they traditionally do in this garden, but the masses of artemisia, sedum, pennisetum and alchemillas are the path edgings of a more modern taste and style. (August)*

maybe because the photographers never turned out at the right time of brilliant flowering, but those brief moments of the roses were stunning. Those arching sprays, those fountains of pinks, maroon velvets, blushing creams, wine-crimsons and lavender-mauves thrown skyward by 'Felicia', 'Moonlight', 'Madame Lauriol', the Cardinals, Commandants, Souvenirs, 'Madame Pierre Oger', 'Zérphirine Drouhin' and all their splendid company must have been the loveliest sight Sissinghurst ever offered.

Besides the importance of Vita's roses as the expression of an advanced 'thirties' taste (it was a taste shared with Constance Spry, who proceeded to launch it upon the whole fashionable world of flowers after the War), the rose garden was her special garden. If Harold re-fashioned his 'alpine meadow of a life' in his lime walk, and the White Garden expresses their joint effort, then the essence of Vita's personality is most evident here. The rose garden was made on the site of the old Tudor garden, on the south side of the house (as at Knole) and she quickly appropriated this historic plot as surely as she bagged 'her' tower. The Rondel and its oasthouse origins, unearthed when she was writing *The Land*, were her tribute to her beloved Kent countryside. Her roses filled her poetry. She was, she admitted 'drunk on roses', they were the highlight of her gardening year and she was never far from the rose garden in their flowering season. She sang their praises, she cursed them, she worked hard for them – all the things one does for and with beloved offspring; and, when they had their fling, she too, had had enough. They suited her; by the time their flowering was over she was invariably bored of her garden. She did not like the blowsy heaviness of July, and by the middle of the month she was invariably gone far away, to Europe or to look at other peoples' gardens elsewhere in England. Thus the rose garden, far more than any other part of Sissinghurst, even the White Garden, expresses the essence of Vita's gardening personality, just as her writing-room enshrines her poetic ghost.

Above *A closer view of* Euphorbia characias wulferii *'Lambrook Gold' filling the empty window frame of old Sissinghurst's Tudor house. Vita knew this plant and realized it was a serious lapse on her part not to grow it; she called it 'the most recommendable of the spurges'. (March)*

Opposite *A general view of the rose garden showing autumn afternoon light on the last roses of summer. Mallows, sedum heads, rose heps and, in the foreground, Osteospermum 'Pink Whirls' provide the end of season colouring. The curious white fruits are on the young* Sorbus cashmiriana, *which had soft pink blossom in May. It is a native of Kashmir, as its name implies, and highly appropriate for this garden, a repository of so many plants symbolic of Vita's passion for the Orient. (October)*

Above *The south side path of the rose garden newly paved in Tudor-style bricks, used laid on-edge for the path edging. A large splash of* Verbena 'Sissinghurst' *a new introduction named in honour of the garden, grows on the right. Mallows now play an important part in the later flowering of this garden, including the very popular* Malvia thuringiaca 'Barnsley' *named for Mrs Rosemary Verey's garden in Gloucestershire where it was first grown. (August)*

Right *The extreme south-east bed of the rose garden in spring shows the structure which holds the later flowers. The hazel hoops or 'benders' are cut from the nuttery. They are green and pliable when freshly cut and curve satisfactorily when stuck into the soil; the rose branches are tied to them in the autumn, ready to support the shoots and display the flowers the following season. (March)*

THE
LIME WALK AND
THE NUTTERY

The nuttery and the lime walk represent the old and the new at Sissinghurst; the copse of hazel trees was the best planting that the Nicolsons inherited when they bought their garden, and the lime walk was made as a wholly new feature, by taking in land from the lake field, and thus forming a double composition. It was a composition born of obstructed dreams, for they realized that it was impossible to have a lime walk as they wanted around the southern boundary of the garden, because the hazels were in the way; and yet the lines of hazels did not conform to a hoped-for vista through from the rose garden to the moat either. The result was therefore an English compromise, though with no tinge of mediocrity.

The discovery of the nuttery had clinched their decision to buy Sissinghurst. They had

Opposite *The nuttery in spring.*
Above *The cottage garden, lime walk and nuttery seen from the tower. (October)*

visited the Castle separately at first, and then made their second excursion together, on 6 April 1930. Harold recorded what happened in his diary: 'My anxiety had been that the main wing would be too narrow to build in. But we measure and find that we get 18 feet. We then go round the buildings carefully and finally walk round the fields to the brook and round by the wood. We come suddenly upon a nut walk and that settles it...'. To understand why the nut walk was so important it is only necessary to recall Vita's passionate affection for the Kent countryside and all its traditions, and that in these the Kent cobnut played a great part. The very existence of the hazels was a treasure in terms of countryside economy, for their nuts or alternatively for the regular coppicing of their highly prized rods for making wattle hurdles and for hoops for cider barrels. Coppicing, the cutting at intervals of the hazel shoots down to the ground, is one of the oldest traditions of English woodlands; it had thrived for a thousand years, and despite the city-based values of the twentieth century still survives today. Finding the hazels was like finding the moat wall – a legacy from a distant heyday. It was also one gleam of foresight and good management in the complete dereliction and decay of Sissinghurst in 1930. These hazels must have been planted by the previous owners, the Barton Cheesmans or the Wilmshursts, in response to a revival for them in Edwardian England. Hazel coppices have such great garden merits and value that it became customary to plant them within the boundaries of large gardens, safe from the ravages of cattle, and more conveniently to hand than when grown in oak woods. The nut walk was an early Edwardian version of wild gardening, and soon their garden advantages became clear; the hazel catkins offered the first sign of spring, even in the midst of winter, and then the copse was the natural habitat for primroses and bluebells. In summer the walks were cool glades and then in autumn they glowed when the leaves turned to gold. After the nuts came the cutting, which provided rose hoops, sticks for peas and beans and brush for staking shrubs and herbaceous perennials; under snow, the neat avenues reminded the poetically-minded not so much of icy cathedrals as chilly aisles of Norman churches. All these considerations tumbled into that one phrase of Harold's – 'We come suddenly upon a nut walk and that settles it...'.

When they found it, it was naturally brambly, overgrown and weedy. It was cleared as a priority, along with the digging out of the moat wall. After heaps of rubbish had been carted away and many a bonfire burned, the levels were adjusted: the low level moat walk was necessary to show off the beauty of the old wall, so the surplus soil made up the parallel bank, which protected the nut trees from any change of level in their ground.

From the hazel copse as a natural habitat for primroses it was not a great step to assume that it would make a colourful garden for polyanthus, and to have such a polyanthus garden was one of the most treasured ideals of Edwardian gardeners. The Nicolsons would have seen the idea in the country house travels of their youth, and Vita saw Gertrude Jekyll's nut walk which led from the north side of Munstead Wood house, between flower and shrub borders, and was underplanted with cheerful red and orange polyanthus. Miss Jekyll was also largely responsible for rescuing polyanthus from obscurity in the 1880s, and her Munstead strains of yellow and cream flowers were grown separately in her primrose garden on the other side of the house.

Like many other gardeners Vita was particularly fascinated by the primula, polyanthus and auricula varieties for their complex histories, and their generous natures in producing so many deliciously coloured and patterned blooms on a single sturdy stem, like little jewelled trees. She treasured auriculas in special corners of the garden, and in pots, and grew the taller, damp loving primulas, *Primula japonica*, *P. bulleyana* and *P. florindae* beside the moat and in the damp corner of the tower lawn where the Lion Pond had been. She particularly admired the Bartley strains of *Primula pulverentula* raised by

Polyanthus of the Barnhaven strain growing in the lime walk. These many coloured strains were revived at the Barnhaven Nursery in Cumbria. (March)

the Dalrymple brothers at the House-in-the-Wood near Southampton, and she also made a modest collection of the Elizabethan primroses with amusing names, jack-in-the-green and the hose-in-hose flowers. Quite characteristically it was this flower of old England aspect that appealed so much; polyanthus – in the various quaint spellings of their names – belonged to floras and herbals of the mid-seventeenth-century, where they were also called 'false oxlip' from their parentage of wild primroses and cowslips. Once discovered they were enthusiastically taken up and produced in shades of orange, red and maroon, almost black, and then with the fancy gold-lacing around the petal edges that the florists loved. By the eighteenth century they were a show and florists' flower and almost, but not quite, of equal status with auriculas, but the popularity of the lace-edged flowers apparently drove the old gold and yellow strains (on which the lacing did not show) into the dimmest corners of cottage gardens. It was Miss Jekyll's discovery of a

The lime walk: the lime trees were originally planted in 1932 (the ones in this photograph are the replacements planted in 1974) and flanked by hornbeam hedges to make a green avenue approach to the nuttery. The only ornaments to this green walk were some large and very smooth Italian terracotta jars which Harold ordered in Italy before the War. During the Second War he conceived the idea of making the walk into a spring garden. He carefully planned the planting to go around each tree using mixtures of spring flowers and constantly reviewed the different effects. (May)

83

A typical patch of lime walk planting in full flowering. Harold's intention was to make 'an alpine meadow' of a garden in memory of the varied life he had lived. Here tiny yellow Poet's daffodils, grape hyacinths, white Anemone appennina, orange and pink tulips and scarlet polyanthus crowd together in just the way he intended. (March)

pale cream 'bunch primrose' in a Surrey cottage garden (which she crossed with a named polyanthus 'Golden Plover' to produce her Munstead varieties of creams, yellows and gold) that reintroduced the colourings we now know. After Miss Jekyll, commercial nurserymen produced some familiar red, orange and purple strains; Vita bought some of her polyanthus from stock held by Scotts of Merriot in Somerset.

The Sissinghurst polyanthus, with their pedigree coming from shade-loving primroses and sun-loving cowslips, were thus ideally suited to the nuttery, where the shade became more dappled as the sun gained in strength during their spring flowering. The natural leafy woodland floor was carefully retained, and they were given generous helpings of farm manure. In this way the seedlings flourished and soon covered first one of the nuttery aisles, and then the others. They came into full flower, a gloriously coloured carpet of yellows, creams, gold, salmon, pinky-orange, orange, scarlet, maroon, violet and cerise, all softened like faded tapestry colours because of the interleaving of green, for that first year that the visitors came, 1938. This cheerful and enchanting sight, seen from the nuttery path with its edging of sweet woodruff, must have been a precious memory to so many of the Nicolsons' friends and visitors. Harold called it 'the loveliest planting scheme in the whole world', this heart-warming company of the bright and the good, lit by the morning sun slanting through the hazels, a garden of hope that persisted in blooming in the face of oncoming war.

The very severe winter of 1939–40 must have hit the polyanthus hard, and by the time they bloomed in the spring of 1940 all thoughts of creative gardening at Sissinghurst had been abandoned. Vita, pre-occupied with blacking-out and air-raid shelters and the chores of keeping her little community going by day, had taken to poetry and prose as her means of fighting. Harold, as a Member of Parliament working for the Ministry of Information and living through the London blitz, relegated his garden to the realms of sweet dreams where it was an occasional luxury in a world of nightmares. He was deeply distressed and depressed by the War – they both were – for many and complex reasons which cannot be included here. But the outcome was that they both dreamed of their garden, and privately resolved that – if ever it was all over – their garden would be made more beautiful than ever. Sissinghurst was a powerful motive for survival and throughout the limbo-land of the seasons from 1940 to the spring of 1945, they looked

Opposite *Tulips 'Red Shine' with forget-me-nots in one of the terracotta urns which decorate the lime walk. (May)*

Left *The nuttery path. At this time of year, at the end of May, with the azaleas in flower along the moat walk, the canopy of the hazels holds in their scent. Beside the path is a woodland covering of the shade loving Geranium sylvaticum* 'Mayflower', *Trillium grandiflorum, ferns, Omphalodes cappadoccia and Euphorbia robbiae. (May)*

Below *A group in the lime walk of Tulipa purissima and* Leucojum aestium, *summer snowflake. (March)*

Above *'Apricot Beauty' tulips in the lime walk. Tulips of all varieties have always been grown here in rich profusion and in elegant contrast to soft carpets of forget-me-not and grape hyacinths. (April)*

Right *The nuttery in June;* Hosta tokudama, Dactylorhiza × grandis, *ferns and* Epimedium pubigerum *beside the path.*

Below *The young god on his plinth in the nuttery. He and his companion (opposite) gaze at each other down the green avenues of hazels and limes; for all we know they may meet beneath the full moon and return to their plinths by morning. Vita saw these two statues from the top of a London bus travelling down the Euston road; she got off immediately, rushed back and ordered them to be sent to Sissinghurst.*

back on what they had achieved and forward to what they might do. But this enforced break in garden-making, when though the garden suffered from lack of sufficient attention, it also carried on growing to maturity, was not entirely damaging. Sissinghurst in its post-war phase was to benefit from this long contemplation.

The lime walk, made as an elegant, paved green walk between hedges and the pleached limes, was perfectly fulfilled when the nuttery flowered. This composition exactly expressed the desired effect of expectation and surprise. But, slowly, out of the depressions of war, it seems that Harold changed his mind about this particular part of the garden. Maybe the polyanthus suffered very badly in those wartime winters? Maybe he felt they would never find or afford the time and labour to plant them again? And then, it is a strange truth of human nature, that when tragedy befalls people or places that we think we don't particularly care about, it comes as a shattering blow, and this is how Harold reacted to war-time Berlin. He had spent two and a half years there in the late twenties; it was his last diplomatic posting. He had crammed what seemed like a decade of activities into that time, besieged by hard work and invasions of friends who wanted to be entertained in Sally Bowles' city, in those last frantic months of the Weimar Republic. It had been exciting, but he had grumbled that Berlin was so 'third-rate' – but then it was also familiar, an old friend. He was deeply upset by the bombings, the loss of life and the loss of irreplaceable buildings. (When he saw the ruins of Berlin in 1948 it was 'a nightmare fusion of the recognizable and the changed, just as if one were to come upon Knole in ruins upon Salisbury Plain', he told Vita.)[1] His private memory of the city he had known came into his garden and he called his lime walk *Unter den Linden* after the famous avenue. After the deep disappointment of losing his parliamentary seat in the July 1945 election, he vowed he would devote his time to making his lime walk into the 'loveliest spring border' – an alpine meadow of a border – and he christened this endeavour 'My Life's Work' or MLW.

The Bacchante, or young goddess, with the cymbals on her plinth, at the head of the lime walk.

Harold's purposefulness made his lime walk the most lavishly recorded of Sissinghurst's gardens, with every idea set out in meticulous detail in notebooks which he began in 1947 and continued through until the late fifties. Harold's 'Life's Work' had its own allowance to pay its gardener, Sidney Neve, and to finance his constant scouring of the Royal Horticultural Society's monthly shows for new and likely plants. He also came to terms with weeding, doing regular stints on Saturday afternoons; on one notorious occasion – almost cause for a divorce – he poisoned Vita's carefully made compost heap with MLW's crop of creeping buttercup. After his weeding, he would retire to his desk in the window of the South Cottage, and modify his plans; armed with blue and red biros, lead and red pencils, he marked out the trees and numbered them one to fifteen on squared paper. Around each tree he made notes – what was there, what was good and what was not, what was to be moved elsewhere, and what it would be nice to add for next year. His notebooks are a cavalcade of ideas: small crowds of his favourite daffodils, 'Mrs R. O. Backhouse', the pink daffodil, and *Narcissus bulbocodium conspicuus*, the 'hooped petticoat' – with jonquils. (About the jonquils he had written to Vita from London on an occasion of discovery before the War: 'you have no idea how I love them. I never thought of them much before – little meagre yellow things that I was never allowed to pick, then in an orgy of recklessness you put at least 7 jonquils into my

Monday bouquet, and they smell out the whole Strand and across the river to Oxo, they shout in thin little voices . . . and the whole of spring and Sissinghurst settles on King's Bench Walk'.)[2]

Thus came about the planting of jonquils in this garden of memories. And there are more memories – delicate soft yellow *Tulipa* linifolia (Batalinii) mixed with *Sparaxis* 'Fire King', *Anemone* De Caen and a patch of pinky-white myosotis. He loved the Cottage tulips, and included 'Couleur Cardinal' (hence its traditional planting in the Cottage garden's copper) and Cottage Beauty, the frail Lady Tulip, *Tulipa clusiana*, and the old favourite 'Clara Butt'. Each lime tree had its company of flowers, but lime tree no. 7 north was once a 'museum piece' of success, surrounded by *Anemone fulgens*, jonquils and dog's tooth violets. The large terracotta jars along the walk, which he had brought from Italy before the War, were planted with *Clematis macropetala*, so that its tendrils and violet-blue flowers tumbled out of the jar and mixed with small iris and muscari that ran between the pavings, with *Gentiana acaulis* and even the small winged Genoa broom, *Genista januensis*. He grew the old polyanthus – the jack-in-the-green and hose-in-hose plants that Vita would give him – along with auriculas and *Omphalodes luciliae* from her sink gardens. He tried a planting of *Primula denticulata*, which the gardener Neve was instructed to swamp with the new snake irrigation. The whole meaning of Harold's Life Work was its endless variety; no two patches of flowers were duplicated, endless variety was the theme of his life, a life like 'an alpine meadow patinated with the stars of varied flowers'. ('Would I feel happier if I had stuck to a single crop of lucerne or clover?' he had asked himself – and, fortunately for the lime walk, answered 'No'.)[3] There was a 'very pretty section' between limes 4 and 5 north of tulips, fritillaries, *Omphalodes*, narcissus and anemones. And there were his coveted Parrot tulips 'enamelled like Battersea china' which induced him into a flurry of extravagant ordering at the flower shows. For Harold, his Life's Work became an intensely-pursued hobby, patiently and regularly attended to; like so many keen gardeners he gave the impression of much concern over his little flowers and their welfare, whether this year was better than the last (it was invariably worse), whether this or that frost would be devastating and cause absences amongst the 'little green noses' of March, or simply whether he was being over-extravagant. All such thoughts contributed to his enjoyment. Vita never interfered, but she did keep an eye on progress if he was away; she reported on her tour of inspection one day in March 1952, whilst he was in Greece – 'not very much is happening owing to the lack of sun, but lots of little noses, many of which I don't recognize – two of your Kaufmanniana tulips at the foot of the statue are showing colour and two Dog's Tooth Violets are open . . . the primroses look well and there are lots of little cups of crocuses between the paving stones . . . everything is quite incredibly tidy and there is masses of manure everywhere, which rejoices my heart because it usually goes on William's cabbages'.[4] (William Taylor was in charge of the vegetable garden; no vegetable's have been grown at Sissinghurst since 1963.)

The MLW notebooks carry on until the late fifties; perhaps they stop because so many desired effects had been achieved and success confirmed, or perhaps it was that Vita's health gave him cause for worry, but the zest seemed to go out of this hobby. The double composition of the many-flowered lime walk leading to the multi-coloured carpet of the nuttery polyanthus had been restored after the War, as Harold had vowed he would, and had flowered with brilliant success. Then tragedy struck in the nuttery, as Vita bemoaned to her *Observer* readers in the autumn of 1960; first the border of sweet woodruff sickened and died, and despite all her best efforts at diagnosis and treatment, she could not revive it. Next, the polyanthus weakened as the divided plants and new seedlings failed to thrive. She remembered the thick borders that used to go on flowering from year to year in old

Opposite *Autumn crocus at the feet of the glowing azalea leaves beside the nuttery path. (October)*

Harvest time in the nuttery when the warm colours of the hazel leaves turn the aisles and walks into patterns of greens and gold. (October)

kitchen gardens – were they not so happy in the hazel copse after all? Well, perhaps quite so many years in old gardens was a myth, or perhaps Sissinghurst was just unfortunate. It is known that occasionally soil-borne diseases can build up over a long period and weaken the plants, and signs of disease – failing and rotting root systems and a brown core in the crown – mean that the plant must be removed and burned. For many years, during the sixties, this was the regime for the nuttery; the careful inspection of plants for disease and their replacement with healthy seedlings, and the addition of loads of manure and bonemeal fertilizer. This kept the magic carpet flowering until 1974, but then the Trust was forced to make one of the hardest decisions about Sissinghurst – to give up even trying to grow the polyanthus carpet. It was a decision that deeply upset so many regular visitors, especially those who had known Vita and Harold; they came in 1975 and found the nuttery changed; other visitors, coming especially to see the garden's most famous spring sight, asking expectantly 'Where are the polyanthus?' went away disappointed. It was like a death in the family. Perhaps it is a salutary lesson to those who design complex planting schemes, that this simplest of ideas could win so many hearts and fuel so many happy memories. Perhaps it also seems impossible that modern, scientific gardening cannot overcome such a known quantity as soil disease. But evidently it cannot, and the only possible way to bring back the polyanthus to Sissinghurst would be to change completely the soil of the nuttery, which cannot be done without destroying the nut trees themselves.

So now the nuttery shelters a quite different and often very beautiful woodland garden. At the end of winter the first signs of life lift from beneath the nut-brown carpet of leaves – bright anemones and uncurling ferns. In April, when the lime walk is a cavalcade of colour, the nuttery is luminous spring green, from the light that filters through the young hazel leaves on to the young ferns, blue myosotis and sprouting euphorbias. In summer the richly textured carpet of varying greens is coloured with lilies and a sprinkling of yellow Welsh poppies. On the hottest days the path through here offers a welcome shady walk, and the whole feeling of the copse is of green-shaded aisles, quite different from any other part of the garden. In late summer, when the green light changes to a gold and russet-tinted glow it is quite a different place again, especially magical when the afternoon sun slants through the hazels and lights the dappled floor.

Though change has been forced on the nuttery planting, and the polyanthus are a sight greatly missed, the nut trees are in good heart. Their way of life, constant thinning and constant renewal of the nut-bearing branches, means that they will carry on as long as the stools are healthy. In their green guise of spring, with the luminous carpet of ferns and woodruff, the nut walks offer a fine and magical compliment to the lime walk in full spring flower. This now has its turn, and quite rightly, to be the highlight of Sissinghurst's spring. Part of its magic is just that sense of surprise which Harold delighted to contrive. It can be indulged in every year, especially by those visitors who come to the garden for the first time; their curiosity is sated in the courtyard, then they explore the tower and the tower lawn, wander into the rose garden and admire the hedges and modest display, and then – intrigued by the glimpse of the Bacchante, follow the green corridor to her, not unlike Alice peering into the distant prospect of the magical garden. When they reach Bacchante and turn round they often gasp – even the most self-controlled of them – for it is *such* a wonderful way to plant a garden. Splashes of vivid orange and scarlet polyanthus and tulips, rivers of blue muscari and violas, tiny winged narcissi which look as if they are about to fly away, nodding fritillaries, starry anemones – memories of alpine meadows, a hint of the desert flowering after rain; all these images come flooding in to this corner of an English garden, exactly as Harold wished.

Surrounded by falling leaves the Bacchante at the head of the lime walk plays on, flanked by the survivors of Harold's terracotta oil jars filled with elegant sprays of Coronilla glauca *'Citrina'. (October)*

THE
COTTAGE GARDEN,
THE CRESCENT AND
THE MOAT WALK

If the rose garden was Sissinghurst's *grand salon*, then the garden in front of the South Cottage was the Nicolsons' private sitting-room – 'our own little garden' was the way in which they regarded it. The South Cottage is picturesque and tiny, almost square, with a central front door and rooms either side. It is of soft brick, with tiled roof and oak doors and window frames; Vita liked to think that it still had touches of distinction that befitted this only surviving fragment of the Bakers' courtyard. When they found it, it was in a neglected condition; they cleaned up the outside and covered it with roses. Inside they had to remove heavy layers of wallpaper, unblock fireplaces, windows and doors, and carefully replace floorings and other woodwork. The work was all done with great care by the builders Beale & Son from Tunbridge Wells, under the supervision of Dick Beale,

Above Helleborus orientalis *beside the path leading to the orchard. (March)*
Opposite *The South Cottage clad in rose 'Madame Alfred Carière'. (June)*

Above *The south front of the South Cottage, with the new single yellow rose 'Helen Knight' making her way up the wall at the east corner. The borders below the windows are filled with their traditional spring planting of wallflowers,* Cheiranthus *'Fire King'. (May)*

Below Erysimum *'Bowles Variety', the wallflower which truly loves to sprout from the hot dry wall, where it was one of Vita's original plants. It was named after the gardener and botanical artist E. E. Bowles, who raised it in his garden at Myddelton House in Enfield, London. (March)*

and it was accomplished in the best vernacular manner (of which the Society for the Protection of Ancient Buildings would have most thoroughly approved) with a definite lack of pretension and glamour.

Once finished their cottage provided them with a bedroom each upstairs, Vita's on the right, Harold's on the left. Downstairs, there was a sitting-room on the right and Harold's writing-room on the left. The furniture was what was necessary, mostly polished oak and comfortable arm chairs; it was old, of course, and complemented the pictures and tapestries and had come from Knole's attics, from Vita's antique hunting expeditions with her mother or from Lady Sackville herself. Both Vita and her mother had a good eye for furniture, but Vita was not really interested; as long as something was Jacobean, or looked like it, she cared little how battered or tattered it became, and the indoor-rooms at Sissinghurst changed far less than the garden-rooms. But the South Cottage did have some very good rugs, 'museum carpets' as Harold called them, from France or Persia, gifts from Lady Sackville. And plenty of books, on shelves made for them, against every spare piece of wall.

The Sissinghurst regime began at the South Cottage. On weekdays, when Harold was in London, Vita would rise at about eight o'clock (it was her persistent claim that she would get up when she woke, but invariably like all of us, she fell asleep again) and emerge to inspect the garden *en route* to breakfast in the Priest's House at nine. After breakfast she wrote until lunch; afternoons were usually eventful, and she liked to do her serious gardening in the late afternoon, after her gardeners had finished. A bath and change, and drinks at the South Cottage preceded the walk to dinner. Hence the garden of the South Cottage fitted this pattern – it was to be there, cheerfully waiting for its occupants to greet the morning, and it was there, ready again, glowing in the early evening; in the morning the rising sun splashed the Irish yews, and in the evening the setting sun gave the 'sunset colours' of Vita's flowers a wonderful glow.

The South Cottage was a modest establishment, and they loved it dearly, which is an interesting comment upon their unusual personalities. Vita may have been brought up in the largest private house in England, and Harold may have often wished that they had invested in a classical eighteenth-century house with elegant Georgian rooms, a drive and double gate lodges (as he often did in bad moments) but they were both completely happy with the South Cottage. It did, after all, have advantages; they had, singly or together, complete privacy, and the question of guests, or even of sleeping within sound of their children or servants, did not arise. It was peaceful, there were no kitchen or front hall activities, these were all elsewhere, and it was certainly the most comfortable of the Sissinghurst venues. The little garden had sun all day, and though Vita was hardly ever given to sitting in her garden, this is where she might occasionally come to rest; but it was more a matter of idle weeding, the perfect place to pass a spare ten minutes, in the sun, out of the wind, attending to the comfortable kinds of plants that belonged here.

The South Cottage has a cottage garden – an idea much in vogue in the 1930s. But what did the Nicolsons mean by a cottage garden? Surely, with lives spent in great houses, Mayfair, Florence and Constantinople, they cannot have known too many. Harold's taste was very definitely for the Georgian and classical – he did not enjoy vernacular lifestyles. Vita would have been horrified to have it suggested that she was doing a middle-class thing, and smartening up the former dwelling of some long dead rustic so that she could play at country living, for this was the reason for cottage garden revivals at that time. And anyway, the South Cottage was really the former home of some long dead noble! Arguably, Sissinghurst as they had found it had been a whole series of 'real' cottagers' gardens, with the odd rose and michaelmas daisy surviving amongst rows and rows of cabbages. The sound sociological idea of mixing cabbages and

Above *A view from the orchard side of the moat wall, across the white wisteria flowers to the flowers of the azalea bank. (May)*

Left *The moat wall in spring. This interesting photograph shows how the wall is obscured on the orchard side, where the photographer is standing, and where a ribbon of blue* Symphytum caucasicum *has been planted to contrast with the white wisteria sprouting on top of the wall. Through the wisteria branches can be seen the much lower level of the moat walk, dug down to reveal the bricks and piers of the wall on its southern side. (May)*

Following page *The white* Wisteria floribunda *'Alba' in full flower on the moat wall. (June)*

flowers in a cottage garden was certainly not what they had in mind.

In the end, the most direct route to Vita's idea of a cottage garden seems to come from the Victorian garden critic, William Robinson. Though she would only grudgingly acknowledge that Gertrude Jekyll might have had any influence upon her gardening, it was quite the opposite with the irascible, cantankerous old Irishman, whom she both adored and admired. She paid him one memorable visit at Gravetye Manor in 1928, tolerating a terrifying lurching progress around his woods in his electric cart; he was nearing ninety, and he had written to congratulate her on *The Land*, a letter which she treasured, and she paid him generous tribute in one of her *Country Notes*.[1] She also treasured, and read, his *English Flower Garden* and *The Wild Garden*, and actually, it is in these two wonderful books that many of Sissinghurst's planting ideas will be found. For the moment, from the first chapter of the *English Flower Garden*[2] Robinson writes: 'What is the secret of the cottage garden's charms? Cottage gardeners are good to their plots, and in the course of years they make them fertile. The shelter too, of the little house and hedge favours the flowers. But there is something more. It is the absence of any pretentious pattern which lets the flowers tell their story to the heart. The walks are only what are needed, and so we see only the earth and its blossoms'.

Robinson would approve of the cottage garden's simple layout, which is basically of quartered beds centred on a crossing, and all the paths, which were made in crazy pavings of found-fragments of stone with bricks, are functional. The focal point has a suitably bucolic ornament, a large, battered verdigris copper, which Vita found lying in a farmyard and brought home in triumph. It is now something of a treasure, being of real copper, whereas the far more common successors turned out of laundry rooms are cast iron, and less attractive. William Robinson would probably also have smiled at the four Irish yews, a flourish of the warm south, in this very English setting.

Thus the cottage garden has the fertility, the shelter and the lack of pretension that Robinson would allow. But what of the flowers? Vita did not go scouring country lanes and raking over cottage gardens as Gertrude Jekyll had done and Margery Fish would do for her book *Cottage Garden Flowers* (1961), for there was no need. Cottage garden plants were a perfectly recognizable group within her mind. Her knowledge of literature and history, her passion for Shakespeare and flowers, and for herbs and their names, all made her aware of the columbines, mignonette, snapdragons, carnations, sweet williams, lilies, peonies, love-in-a-mist, hollyhocks, roses and gillyflowers of Elizabethan England. She had a fine gardener's sense for plants that were 'easy' – tough, divided or grown from cuttings, and those that happily seeded themselves in just the right places. She had an even finer sense for the social ordering of plants, of those that were aristocrats and those that were humble. Unless one does have it, this is very difficult to define; it is something akin, I suppose, to a perfumier's 'nose' or a gourmet's palette, and it is something that tends to change with fashion. Colour also has much to do with this class distinction amongst flowers – some aristocrats can be cool, aloof and difficult (delphiniums, eremurus, Solomon's seal, agapanthus) and how can royal purples and maroon, a black tulip or *Lobelia cardinalis* be anything but noble? Sunny yellows and golds, on the other hand, Nature's easiest colours, are boisterous and good-hearted. When Vita allotted her garden's colourings, she was instinctively getting it right; by choosing sunset colours for her cottage garden she was in tune with a jovial, salt-of-the-earth crowd of geums, sun roses, snapdragons, achilleas, day lilies, pansies, poppies, golden mints and thymes, nasturtiums, red hot pokers and evening primroses. Herbs could well have been included, for colour and social connections, but these were to be grown elsewhere.

Cottage gardening also – to Vita and many others – symbolized lavishness, a small space bursting with flowers. Anne Scott-James has observed in her book *The Cottage*

Above *A view across the centre of the cottage garden with the columbines, yellow achilea 'Moonshine' and tawny irises. (June)*

Below *A long-spurred hybrid aquilegia in the sunset colours of the cottage garden. (May)*

Garden that Vita's writing on gardening has the words 'romantic', 'profusion' and 'cottagey' occurring over and over again.[3] She continues that 'it would be absurd to suggest that all her plant material was cottagey' and I think this has been made clear in my descriptions of the rose garden and the White Garden above all. But, here, in the cottage garden, restrained and defined by sunset colours, she has turned the Edwardian revival of the cottage garden into a stylish romantic bower. No cottager would have dreamed of refusing a flower because of its colour; the carefree, innocent mixture of every colour was the essence of a cottage garden. Equally, no gardener of fashion this side of the Victorian and Edwardian discovery of colour 'rules' could plant without giving some thought to the subject. This is, therefore, a revivalist cottage garden, for a restored cottage which was filled with books and museum-quality carpets. As such, William Robinson would have wholly approved.

It was also rather romantic as a symbol in the Nicolsons' lives, a source of 'tussie-mussies', a term which Margery Fish's research into cottage flowers explains as follows: 'used for the little bunches of flowers that came from cottage gardens to less fortunate friends living in towns. The spring mixture was bunch-primroses, forget-me-nots and wall flowers, and later in the year the scented pinks and roses were mixed with the striped grass called Gardener's Garters, a few sprays of maidenhair fern or some spikes of lavender'.[4] These 'cottage bo-kays' were a country tradition that went to town, sold from hand carts by the flower ladies of Victorian London. In Sissinghurst's case the 'less fortunate' living in London was, of course, Harold, and returning to town with a mixed offering from the garden was the unchanging ritual of his life. The flowers were customarily gathered by Vita; it was something she had always done and it was one of the reasons for her gardening. She wrote an *Observer* piece on tussie-mussies and was shocked to note that the Oxford Dictionary deemed the term obsolete; she said she had always used it, and would continue to do so. Tussie-mussies began at the beginning of their marriage, when Harold was away; she sent him plants – cuttings and bulbs for his hoped-for garden in Teheran – and then started sending him flowers, packed in cigar boxes. The picking, packing and sending – via a swift diplomatic bag – and their state upon arrival, became a great subject for letter gossip. Once started, the offerings continued, wherever he was. The absence of a tussie-mussie (for which a special basket was made) was a sure sign of a rift in their relationship. He insisted on miserably gathering them for himself after Vita's death.

All these associations make the cottage garden the most intimate and romantic of Sissinghurst's places; it was a shared garden, where they both weeded, and both had a say in the planting, and most of the plants they chose were old familiars. The noisette rose 'Madame Alfred Carrière' that now covers the front of the South Cottage was planted because the same variety climbed to the bedroom windows at Long Barn. In fact this cottage garden was filled with memories of Long Barn, which they had loved so much, while other parts of the Castle and its garden were for grander and newer ideas. Harold admitted that he had 'an elective affinity' for the South Cottage, and this is where he would spend his time when he was at home, often for long periods, concentrating on writing; he was also there at some of the least happy times of his life, as in the thirties when he was anxious about the inevitability of war, and then after the War, when he had lost his House of Commons seat.

In those times, indeed always in Vita and Harold's lifetime, their cottage garden was a little jungle, with its rough and rustic paths almost overgrown with creeping thyme or self-sown pansies and pinks. Many visitors did not intrude, and passed by in their search for the polyanthus in the nuttery; these, with the roses and the White Garden in due season were the real sights of Sissinghurst.

In the cottage garden the colour began with sprays of forsythia and broom (*Genista lydia*) and a favourite witch hazel (*Hamamelis mollis*). On the ground there were patches of yellow and bronze wallflowers, and orangey-bronze ones sprouted from the wall borders of the cottage reflecting more of Vita's *penchant* for 'brown' flowers. In the verdigris copper the traditional first planting is of red tulips 'Couleur Cardinal', a favourite from earliest Long Barn days. The copper is surrounded with shoots of iris, little yellowy spurges and self-sown pansies and primroses; the beds are filled with more purposeful patches of the same. At the end of May everything comes into flower: 'Madame Alfred' covers the wall with her pinky tinged roses and is joined by the yellow flowered Pernet-Ducher rose of the twenties named for 'Lawrence Johnston', the owner of Hidcote Manor in Gloucestershire. Other shrubs adding a golden glow are honeysuckles, *Lonicera* 'Tellmanniana' and *L. tragophylla*, and another broom, *Genista tenera*. Bushing thickly at the path edges are the small shrubby sun-roses, helianthemums which revel in this dry, south-facing garden; they come in marvellous sunny colours, some of them named cultivars, the deep yellow 'Ben Nevis' and self-explanatory 'Coppernob', and in all shades of warm pinks and oranges. After the tulips the copper holds orange *Mimulus glutinosus*, which lasts through till autumn. Around it the jungle

Afternoon shadows in the cottage garden in high summer. The reds are antirrhinum, kniphofias and dahlias, with the red tinge on the leaves of the Canna indica *just visible. Yellow clumps of fennel seed-heads are seen with* Solidago 'Goldenmosa' *and achillea. (August)*

The moat wall in autumn with a ribbon of
Aster × frikartii *'Mönch' along its base, and rich red*
foliage of Cotinus coggyria *in its autumn colouring*
above. (October)

thickens with montbretia, alstroemerias, day lilies, columbines, snapdragons, daisy-like anthemis and plates of gold achilleas. The heat of the colours is not overwhelming, for there is plenty of good greenery; also this was the place for thalictrums (meadow rue), which Vita loved when few other gardeners did, tall stems with fluffy tops of greeny-yellow colour rising from prettily-shaped leaves.

In 1950 alstroemerias were the subject of an *Observer* piece and Vita seemed a little unsure of them; she thought the traditional cottage-garden Peruvian lily almost a weed, but that the new Ligtu hybrids were far more beautiful in coral and buff shades. These, however, should not be mixed with the orange variety – 'Keep the orange away from the coral, for they do not mix well . . . and whoever it was who said Nature made no mistakes in colour-harmony was either colour-blind or a sentimentalist. Nature sometimes makes the most hideous mistakes; and it is up to us gardeners to control and correct them'.[5] She did plant Ligtu hybrids, for they show in later photographs, but clearly the sunset colours needed careful judgement – a finer point of gardening then which is so often overlooked in these days of ubiquitous mixed packets of seeds.

Around the corner of the South Cottage, where the ground slopes to a path leading through to the orchard, there is now some interesting planting. The hedge border beside this path is home for Sissinghurst's Lenten roses, the lovely *Helleborus orientalis*, whose purply flowers welcome spring; as one of Vita's readers informed her, they will last indoors if the cut stems are plunged into nearly boiling water. On the opposite side of the path, on a rather nondescript slope beneath the chimney breast of the sitting-room, there is now a dramatic mixture of contrasting foliages, a mix of old Sissinghurst favourites and new arrivals. An enormous yellow tree peony, *Paeoniadelavayi Ludlowii* is undercarpeted with *Lysimachia nummularia* 'aurea' (Creeping Jenny) and epimediums, and there is a *Phlomis russeliana* with bushy *Lonicera nitida* 'Baggesen's Gold' and many clumps of *Euphorbia characias wulfenii*. There are plants of the crunchy-looking fern, *Polystichum setiferum divisilobum* with *Pulmonaria angustifolia* 'Mawson's Blue', smaller euphorbias, *E. polychroma* 'Major' and the beautifully arching *Smilacina racemosa*. I feel this corner would please Harold's taste immensely, it would tickle his sense of the enjoyment of new things and accord with his wish that the best of these should come to Sissinghurst.

From the centre of the cottage garden there is a long view eastwards down the moat walk to Dionysus; it is not a direct view, as the plan on page 131 reveals; there is a kink in it, which is the reason for Sissinghurst Crescent. But it is very clever, because from the far end of the moat walk one can look back and see the seat on the Crescent's dais neatly flanked by the Irish yews of the cottage garden. The plan also reveals how Harold's original desire for a complete vista from the far end of the rose garden to the moat was thwarted by Sissinghurst's obtuseness, but how he arranged his lime walk parallel to the moat wall, at a distance from it, and with a semblance of single purpose in all the paths.

The moat wall is one of the most important fixed – and very firmly fixed – features of the garden. Its strange angle emanates from its age; it must have been part of the earliest house on the site, the medieval manor house of the de Berhams which preceded the Bakers' great house. In the manner of the buildings at Ightham Mote, it may have

Here the Canna indica *is in full flower, showing what a marvellous plant it is, along with the golden rod and orange* Dahlia 'Brandaris'. *(August)*

supported stone and timber-framed buildings; and here, as at Ightham, it originally stood in water. When the Nicolsons found Sissinghurst this wall was almost buried in rubbish and brambles; its revelation, for Vita, was like finding treasure, especially when the substantial bases of the piers were discovered. Its antiquity made it precious and dictated that it needed little ornamentation and should be enhanced only by a plain grass-walk along its length. It was a perfect example of their partnership in the making of the garden – Vita determined the priority, Harold made it work with his clever geometry. A problem arose with the change of level between the nuttery and the moat walk, and the solution was to mask the bank with a covering of azaleas; this was a beautiful piece of asymmetrical planning. When the azaleas were grown and in flower, or even with their bank of soft greenery, the balance between the hard line of the wall and the soft parallel of the flower-covered bank made a vista of complete satisfaction, as seen from the Crescent. The final touch was in the placing of Dionysus beyond the moat, so that he closes this vista; he further ties the garden together by closing the view across the orchard.

The moat wall was beautiful in itself, but needed a little enhancement so Vita planted purple wallflowers in its crevices. As can be seen in the photographs, the addition of the white wisteria, *W. floribunda* 'Alba', was a magical touch. Even across thirty years Luisa Vertova Nicolson has a memory of this magic which makes it even more vivid – 'I remember how pleased she was one morning when she spotted a blooming red and purple wallflower, selfsown in a crevice of a brick wall behind a bush covered with white flowers; she brandished her secateurs and made it shine through the white flowers ... I vividly remember, after so many years, Vita's thoughtful look and deft cutting. She reminded me of a painter at his easel'.[6]

From a list she made for labels for the azaleas it is possible to know what were originally planted; they were old Ghent hybrids in shades of red, flame and orange, highly scented and mixed with *A. Rhododendron calendulaceum*, a vivid orange azalea with particularly brilliant autumn red colouring. Now the earlier flowering is of the well-known fragrant yellow azalea, *Rhododendron luteum*. The scent of these azaleas, undercarpeted with sprouting clumps of hostas and orange-scented *Houttuynia cordata* is very much part of the present pleasure of the moat walk; it wafts across to the seat in Sissinghurst Crescent, where couples of all ages tend to sit close together and gaze down the green vista to Dionysus. It is a very restful view, the green ribbon and the old wall in partnership, with the magnificent frilling of the white wisteria in May, or the late-summer band of mauvy michaelmas daisies at the wall's foot.

The Crescent is not perhaps quite an official name at Sissinghurst; it came about as rather a joke, and a rather undemocratic one! The space was made as a landing for the steps that came up from the dug out moat walk to the level of the cottage garden. At some time in the late thirties, possibly as part of his duties as the newly elected Member of Parliament for West Leicester, Harold was touring new housing developments, which – in those days – invariably had a 'Crescent' named after a flower or local dignitary. He came home with the idea that every self-respecting development must have a crescent also, and so Sissinghurst Crescent was born. Perhaps this is also where Vita's presence is most missed, while the poignant evidence of Harold's absence is the pitiful empty chair, where he used to sit in the sun outside the South Cottage's door. With Vita it is the absence most of all of a scent, the scent of incense, *Humea elegans*, a scent from centuries ago, from Catholic and Tudor England, where Sissinghurst, and to a great extent Vita herself, belonged. *Humea elegans*, propagated by her, became the plant of Sissinghurst – or one of the scents – and it is my only memory of the garden from my first visit which must have been in that last summer of her life. She wrote of Humea, of how this Australian native needed sowing in the warmth and keeping away from frost; how six

Below *Not to be outdone by the cotinus on the moat wall, the azaleas on the opposite side of the walk are showing their autumn colour. The neat cones of the Irish yews in the cottage garden rise behind the seat in Sissinghurst Crescent presenting an unusual view of the garden that today still pleases the eye. (October)*

Above *Sissinghurst Crescent from the path leading into the nuttery, and a view across the cottage garden towards the entrance range of buildings. (October)*

The South Cottage seen from the lime walk in autumn, when the colours of Sissinghurst become predominantly bronze, ochre and gold. (October)

seeds would most likely give six plants, which would be set outdoors after the frosts were past, and how the plants preferred the sun, and six would scent the whole garden. Humea likes rich soil, it likes feeding and when it has done its garden duty it will last far too long indoors; its only vice is that some people are violently allergic to it and it brings up a nasty rash (this is why it was given up at Sissinghurst). The scent and the excitement of it were entrancing – 'Visitors walk around sniffing and saying "What is that curious smell of incense"', Vita wrote in 1950: '"One might imagine oneself in an Italian cathedral instead of an English garden" . . . They are quite right. Eventually they track it down to a six- to eight-foot-tall plant, with large, pointed dark green leaves and a branching spike of feathery cedarwood-coloured flowers. It is neither showy nor conspicuous, and nothing but the scent would lead you to it among its more garish companions, such as the delphiniums; yet it is graceful in its growth and well deserves its adjective *elegans*. It makes its influence felt in more subtle ways than by a great splash of colour. It steals across the air as potently and pervasively as the sweet-briar on a damp evening.'[7] It was these poetic touches of surprise and generosity – the *humea elegans* placed in odd corners where people paused – that inspired her visitors' loyalty and affection. Today, Sissinghurst Crescent is a favourite place for visitors to sit in quiet conversation, and admire the ever-changing garden pictures of the moat walk: the azaleas, the white wisterias and the autumn colours of the nuttery bring them back to the garden again and again.

THE ORCHARD, THE HERB GARDEN AND THE LAKE

The apparent jumble of Sissinghurst spaces in the orchard, herb garden and lake, is really a sequence; the herb garden provides a place of rest and contemplation between perambulations of the park-like areas of the orchard and the lake field. A destination, the provision of a place to go, is the prime device of garden planning, whether represented by a distant temple in a Capability Brown park, or, more relevantly in Harold's vision, a garden-room set apart in the Edwardian manner, such as Lutyens's sunken rose garden at Folly Farm in Berkshire. The herb garden provides the eventual destination for the lime walk and the nuttery path and the moat walk, and without it the effect of these three would be frittered away into the looser landscape beyond in a most unsatisfactory manner. But why make a herb garden so far from the house? The answer is that Vita was not interested in cooking; she loved her garden vegetables made into gourmet dishes, and cooked with lots of herbs, but she had no wish, nor talent, for doing such things herself. She grew her herbs for their looks, their lore and their aromas, and for these reasons she

Above Prunus '*Tai-Haku*' in the orchard. (*April*)
Opposite *The orchard in early spring. (March)*

The south end of the moat in winter. This photograph makes a stark contrast with that on page 19 of the same view in autumn; here the bare branches of the old oak trees which line the moat and protect the garden from the east are dark against the bright, cold sky of a winter morning. (March)

Opposite *Spring begins at Sissinghurst: the view from across the moat towards the Castle, to the South Cottage, the tower and the distant oasthouses in the farmyard. On the right, the reddish glow of the polygonum leaves around the Shanganagh column can be seen. (March)*

crowded them into this rich little garden. It was up to Mrs Staples, her cook, to persuade a gardener to plant essential herbs outside the Priest's House kitchen, or to take the long walk to collect the lovage for the salad or the tarragon to go with scrambled eggs.

The orchard trees were already old when the Nicolsons found Sissinghurst in 1930; possibly the fruit had been planted over a hundred years before to feed the Cranbrook parish poor who worked the farm and lived in the Castle ruins. The orchard ground, being the site of the medieval house and a large part of the Bakers' Tudor mansion, is riddled with old foundations, so there was never any idea of it being cultivated for a garden. Vita rather welcomed the old apple trees as she could plant roses to climb up them, and the first famous sight of the orchard in the 1930s was of the noisette rose 'Madame Plantier' making what Graham Stuart Thomas described as 'a curtained crinoline of white blooms for fully 12 feet' around each tree.[1] Enough fruit trees, apples, pears, greengages, plums and cherries were left to supply fruit for the household and for making cider. To these were added some for ornamental blossoms, largely because of the inspiration of a gardening neighbour, the distinguished plant collector, Captain 'Cherry' Collingwood Ingram, who lived at The Grange in Benenden. Vita was fascinated to hear of the cherries he had brought back from Japan, and which he was largely responsible for introducing to English gardeners, who so wholeheartedly accepted them. The most notable of his cherries to grow here is the famous *Prunus* 'Tai Haku', the 'Great White Cherry', a variety he introduced to the Royal Horticultural Society in 1931, and which flowers splendidly at Sissinghurst still.

To Vita's rose crinolines and white flowering cherries must be added Harold's romantic image of what their orchard would be; in October 1937, whilst banished from Sissinghurst to campaign for election in Leicester, he wrote to Vita 'I think your idea of following the path Hayter has made while duck feeding i.e. round the edge, is right, edged with musk roses and iris and winding paths in the middle with dells, boskies,

tangles – in fact, scope for everything but not garden flowers – wild roses, white foxgloves in droves, narcissus in regiments . . .'.[2] On the strength of his mental picture he had ordered twenty musk roses from Edward Bunyard at Allington. The Shanganagh column base, which he brought from Ireland and set in the orchard was also surrounded with roses. And another rose, with small magenta-maroon flowers and yellow stamens, plays a prominent role amongst orchard flowers. This is the rose that Vita found flowering amongst the Sissinghurst rubbish, a *gallica*, given the name 'Sissinghurst Castle', which now grows vigorously in two beds beside the yew walk.

Harold's green paths with boskies and tangles materialized as mown grass paths through rough grass in the thirties, in what we today would call the meadow manner. In the orchard Vita grew her spring flowers, indulging in sweeps of her favourite yellow daffodils and scented narcissus. The daffodils 'Fortune', 'Carlton', 'Golden Harvest' and 'Winter Gold' were all used first for indoor bowls, then planted out in the orchard, approved of and added to by the hundred, along with the double narcissus 'Cheerfulness' and pheasant's eye narcissus. When she could persuade Harold to part with spare bulbs of the soft pinky daffodil 'Mrs R. O. Backhouse' from the lime walk, these too appeared in the orchard grass. And to the more common meadow flora – cowslips, clovers, scillas and campions – Vita added fritillaries, the white *Fritillaria meleagris* as well as the pink 'dusky gridelin' and the strange greeny, black and yellow *Fritillaria pyrenaica*. But most of all she wanted 'seas of gentians' to grow in the orchard; her gentians were the autumn-flowering *Gentiana sino-ornata*, only four inches high, but brilliant blue 'like the very best bits of blue sky landing by parachute on earth'. She mixed *Cyclamen purpurascens* (sgn. *C. europaeum*) with them, as both plants liked semi-shade under the apple trees and generous dressings of peat and leaf mould, and she thought these two one of the happiest associations of flowers. Her orchard gave her pleasure: 'I spent much of yesterday picking apples, with regret because they looked so pretty on the trees. I filled two barrows. I was very happy . . . The gentians were like the Mediterranean at my feet, my thoughts wandered vaguely round and round my new book and Masefield . . . not a poet I greatly love or admire but one line of his comes constantly into my head "The days that make us happy make us wise" . . .'.[3]

Below *The houseleek – sempervivum – which fills the Cospoli bowl, glowing richly in the October sun.*

Right *The herb garden; spires of mullein, orange marigolds and a rich red bergamot make splashes of colour amongst sober sages, thymes and the hyssop around the centre of the garden. The bowl, brought back from Cospoli by the Nicolsons before the First War, now stands on a plinth of radiant tiles set on edge, a favourite device of Edwin Lutyens's, designed by Nigel Nicolson for the re-paving of the garden in the early 1970s. (August)*

It seems rather amusing now, but these two young people of the twenties beau monde were busy and enthusiastic about the making of lavender bags and pot pourri. Vita seemed to spend hours stripping lavender on the terrace at Long Barn and Harold's letters home admonished her for 'not keeping up' the pot-pourri mix; this was presumably all part of the pursuit of the values of the long-dead rustic in their country cottage and part of Vita's obsession with anything that Shakespeare wrote into the literature of flowers. Vita developed this interest into a small herb garden at Long Barn which was superseded by an even larger one at Sissinghurst, where herbs provided the perfect filling for the garden enclosed in the hedge-planting of the thirties beyond the moat walk and the orchard. The fact that this was far away from the kitchen, in the Priest's House garden, was quite irrelevant to Vita. A modest start with about a dozen varieties was made in the late thirties and then during the War the kitchen herbs were kept in a patch of what is now the White Garden. (The White Garden still allows fennels and sages to be close at hand and rosemary was grown as a 'motherly plant' beside every door and gateway.) When Jack Vass returned to Sissinghurst after the War, he found the herb garden completely filled with ground elder; he set to to clear it out, re-divide the beds and plant herbs again and by 1948 there were over sixty varieties. Vita researched these in poetry, through reading Eleanour Sinclair Rohde's *Herbs and Herb Gardening* (which fostered a herb revival when it was published in 1936) and visiting Lady Hart-Dyke's herb garden

The herb garden photographed from the extreme south-eastern corner, which brings many of the varieties of herbs into view. Tall clumps of mullein, fennel and Apothecary's Rose are seen on the right. Through the break in the hedge the small thyme lawns are in flower, and beyond them Dionysus gazes towards the moat. (August)

at Lullingstone Castle in Kent. She collected herbs for their romantic names and historic associations – wormwood, elecampane, woad, Good King Henry; for their sound of mystery – melilot, *Herba barona*, vervain, orris root (*Iris* 'Florentina'); and for a particular virtue – she tracked down twenty-four varieties of thyme and grew at least six of them, because she discovered that 'To smell the thyme' was a phrase used by the Greeks to express a literary elegance of style. As in so many other aspects of her garden, Vita was well in the vanguard of fashion with her interest in herbs, which it is important to remember now that we are accustomed to the present widespread interest in their use in cooking, medicine and cosmetics. She also collected plants that were not acceptable in the flower garden, and yet were fast disappearing from the countryside because of the decline of their traditional uses, such as pennyroyal, germander and purslane.

The Sissinghurst herb garden came into its own at the same time as the White Garden was being 'born', in the late forties and early fifties. Its contents intrigued the garden visitors, especially the male ones, Vita noted, and it still exerts this fascination. Because of their curiosity and history, herbs are of interest even to non-plantsmen, and many earnest question-and-answer sessions and speculations can be overheard from huddles around the peppermint or woad. The herb garden, like the White Garden, has a life of its own beyond the garden as a whole, and appears in books and broadcasts about cooking, healthy living *and* small gardens.

In recent years more varieties have been added so that there are now over one hundred different herbs and medicinal plants crowded into this very small garden. Some intriguing curiosities have arrived, including the liquorice, a green-flowered relative of lupin and laburnum; the shoo fly plant, *Nicandra physaloides*, known as the 'Apple of Peru', with pale violet bell flowers and strange netted brown fruits in October (it is very poisonous); Birthwort, an escapee from old physic gardens, has a fascinating history as an aid to conception and healthy childbirth and its Greek-inspired name *Aristolochia* means 'best birth'. Its form follows function accordingly and Geoffrey Grigson in *The Englishman's Flora* records that 'The greenish-yellow flower, or perianth, constricts into a tube, then opens into a globular swelling at the base. The swelling was interpreted as the womb, the tube as the birth passages. Like helps like; and by the sympathetic magic eventually formalized into a doctrine of Signatures, its childbed function was assigned to Aristolochia in remote antiquity'.[4]

So many of the herb garden plants can summon just this kind of lore, and Vita's fascination with such things formed a very strong part of her interest in the garden. The teazles and giant angelica now grown here have similar histories, a mix of practical use and superstitious belief; the houseleeks which fill the bowl in the centre of the garden which the Nicolsons brought from Cospoli before the First War, have a long pedigree as protectors of the place where they grow, relayed from Ancient Greece and Rome to medieval Kent where they were known as 'sengreen'. The apothecary's rose, the Rose of Provins, has been used for conserves and confections since the days of Joan of Arc, (Vita discovered this when researching for her biography of Joan which was published in 1936) and the original plant was said to have been brought back by a troubadour in the Crusades. With all these legends and histories, hopes and fears, crowded into one little garden, besides the pattern of textures, colours and the aromatic airs, Sissinghurst's herb garden becomes an evocative volume all by itself.

Beyond the herb garden there was a space left at the head of the moat where Vita experimented with various planting ideas. She tried a bed of hollyhocks because she loved their reflection in the moat; but they were beaten down by the wind. She tried a camomile lawn, but this is not as easy to grow as its common tradition suggests and instead contented herself with the camomile seat in the herb garden. The successful idea

The 'chamomile seat' in the herb garden. (October)

was for a Persian carpet of thymes, purple, red and white flowering varieties woven into each other, with a sprinkling of crocus, poet's daffodil and cyclamen. The thyme carpet is renewed every four or five years and protected from too much wear.

Beyond the garden there is a wicket gate into the lake field, which leads through the avenue of Lombardy poplars to the lake. These poplars were among the first plantings at Sissinghurst, contemporaries of those at the entrance, and they were symbolic of the Nicolsons' enthusiasm for the lake, which is perhaps rather forgotten now that it is the least well-known part of Sissinghurst's garden. In 1930 the overgrown, marshy dells they found in the field were of great interest to them; Vita felt these were the hollows from which the brick-making clay for Tudor Sissinghurst had been dug, and Harold was most likely finally persuaded into the whole Sissinghurst project because he had anticipated that he could ride and make a lake there. They spent about £150 in their first winter of ownership having a dam built so that the Hammer stream, which flows through these fields south of the garden, would fill the marshy hollows. This it did admirably; they built steps to swim from and Vita, who did not like swimming, bought a small row-boat from the Army & Navy Stores. The lake was duly stocked with brown trout and immediately, it seemed, was a success and became part of her daily walking ritual. She wrote in *Country Notes* (her pieces for the *New Statesman* collected in 1939) that from its beginning 'the lake has been a delight, revealing a whole region of wild life I had never known before: water birds, water insects, water plants and the general peacefulness of water life. There are few things to compare with this tranquillity of even a small piece of water at any hour of the twenty four, whether at dawn, mid-day, sunset or midnight, spring, summer, autumn or winter. Few things so well adapted to repair the cracked heart, the jangled temper or the uneasy soul . . .'.

The heyday of the lake was during the thirties. Harold, Benedict and Nigel swam in it daily during the summers and they took their friends there to picnic. There were grand ideas for the lake field, which was to be carpeted with spring flowers, given avenues of polyanthus, or delphiniums to spire beside the Lombardy poplars, or to be filled with groves of blossoming trees. For Vita, the lake became a sacred place; her visit was often the highlight of her quiet days at Sissinghurst – on 22 October 1934 she wrote to Harold 'I went down at sunset . . . oh darling, it was so lovely, the water, the ducks and the sunset and the silhouettes of the two big puppies with their ears pricked, listening, waiting . . . these are the things which make me happy . . .'. Then again on 15 February 1935 'It was lovely down by the lake last night. I went down there at sunset and the water was all flushed. The sluice is running like anything . . .'. She became part practical observer of nature, and part poetic dreamer; she bought herself a fishing rod and tried fishing, but eventually decided that she would rather watch the trout sliding through the water than struggling on her line. She began a war with a visiting heron, who left half-devoured trout carcases on the lake banks; she was prepared to pay the £5 fine for shooting this protected bird, but in the end let him have his way. She wrote a *Country Note* on how she tried to rescue one of her Jacob's sheep which her dogs had chased into the water. The beast swam gamely across the lake and got stuck in the shallow, marshy bank on the opposite side; Vita was in hot pursuit in her boat, she lassoo'd it with the boat's painter which she had cut with her fishing knife . . . 'We sat contemplating one another, the sheep and I, I still wishing to fish but entangled instead with this poor tiresome creature . . . it looked at me with vacant eyes; seldom had I seen so unhelpful a victim. We stared at one another, and as we stared it sank lower and lower . . . until its fleece billowed out like a Victorian bathing-dress, filling with water, floating on the surface in woolly flounces . . . I sat back in the boat thinking how ticklish a problem it was ever to help people out of their private difficulties . . .'. To finish the episode, she rolled up her sleeve

The orchard at Sissinghurst; many of the largest and oldest trees were destroyed by the hurricane in 1987 and the storms of 1990, and the orchard is being re-planted, choosing old local varieties of apples. (August)

The moat and Castle on a warm summer evening.
(August 1989, 8.30 pm)

Opposite *The orchard with the first* Colchicum *showing; the beds on the right contain the rose 'Sissinghurst Castle', a magenta-flowered* Gallica *that suckers vigorously, which was found surviving in the ruins in 1930. (August)*

Above *The orchard now has some fine crab apples; this is the famous* Malus *'Golden Hornet', popular with gardeners since the Second War for these abundant golden fruits. (October)*

Left *Meadow saffron* Colchicum autumnale, *particular favourites of Vita's that are still grown in the orchard. (June)*

Following page *The lake in autumn; the making of the lake was Harold's first fulfilled ambition at Sissinghurst and Vita became especially fond of it as a peaceful retreat. For her, however, it was 'violated' during the wartime army occupation and never held the same fascination again. It was rather neglected during Harold and Vita's later years and has recently been revived by Nigel Nicolson and the National Trust. (October)*

and plunged her arm into the mud and water, untangled the sheep's legs, towed it back to the dry bank and landed it – 'the most unexpected fish I ever caught'.

When the War started the peace of her lake and woods became ever more valuable to her. Taking scraps down to feed the swans, watching the firewood being hauled home from the wood, watching the stars, the searchlights and the dogfights over the wood, became a melancholic indulgence that suited her private depression. The lake and the woods figured prominently in her *Country Notes in Wartime* and in the more pensive parts of her epic poem *The Garden*:

> *Now will the water-lilies stain the lake*
> *With cups of yellow, chalices of cream,*
> *Set in their saucer leaves of olive-green*
> *On greener water, motionless, opaque,*
> *– This haunt of ducks, of grebes, and poacher herns.*
> *Now is the stillness deeper than a dream;*
> *Small sounds, small movements shake*
> *This quietude, that deeper then returns*
> *After the slipping of the water-snake,*
> *The jump of trout, the sudden cry of coot,*
> *The elegaic hoot*
> *Of owls within the bordering wood, that take*
> *The twilight for their own.*
> *This is their hour, and mine; we are alone;*
> *I drift; I would that I might never wake.*

As things turned out, this was her epitaph for her lake and woods. The War brought many violations – the army took over the tower for a watchout point, the lawns were cut for hay and air-raid shelters had to be dug in the orchard – but Vita did not really mind about any of these things. She did, however, mind terribly when the army came and dug themselves in to Roundshill Wood, her wood, and drove their tanks all over the primroses and bluebells, muddied the lake's banks and set invasion traps. For Sissinghurst was on the 'invasion route' from the Channel ports to London, and though it is hard to imagine now, there was then a very real certainty that Hitler's armies would march across the fields. Sissinghurst had to play its part in the defence of the capital, but for Vita it was heartbreaking, another example of the thing that hurt her most, the incursion of insensitive strangers into a place she loved. For her, the tanks cutting through her woods and around her lake were on a par of awfulness with the bombing of Knole, which had been hit in February 1944. On 19 December of that year she wrote to Harold: 'I have lost all pleasure in the lake, and indeed in the woods . . . I shall never love the lake or the woods again in the same way as I used to. You didn't understand when I minded the tanks cutting through the wild flowers. I mind about this more than you would believe. It was a thing of beauty now tarnished forever. One of the few things I had preserved against this horrible new world . . .'[5].

Such sensitivity did not detain her for long; she pulled herself together and wrote a book about the Women's Land Army, which was a constant presence around Sissinghurst in wartime. But she kept to her word, and even after the War, the lake and the woods never became the cossetted places they were before. Indeed, in Vita's late years they were neglected, and Harold did not go for his swims any more. It was Nigel, with his affinity for wilder places and natural landscapes, who looked after this corner of Sissinghurst; in 1978 he gave it over to the National Trust. Work is now in hand to make the lake and the woods once again as obviously attractive as the garden's more immediate pleasures.

THE
WHITE GARDEN

In early December 1939 Vita wrote to Harold in London – ' I have got what I hope will be a really lovely scheme for all white flowers – some clumps of very pale pink, white clematis, white lavender, white agapanthus, white double primroses, white anemones, white camellias, white lilies including giganteum in one corner, and a pale peach coloured primula pulverulenta'. Then the War took over her life and she probably never gave it another thought; but that was the beginning of one of the most famous, most loved and most imitated gardens in the world, the small hedged room that is filled with grey and silver leaves and white flowers and is universally known as *the* White Garden.

The White Garden is so celebrated that its origins are easily forgotten. The aerial photograph taken in the summer of 1932 (on page 26) shows how a garden for the Priest's House had been enclosed by the new yew walk hedge. The northern boundary of the garden at the lane, the Priest's House itself and the north wall of the tower lawn were its other boundaries. Part of this wall had survived from the Bakers' house, though it had

Above Lilium longiflorum *in one of the beds of the White Garden. (July)*
Opposite Solanum jasminoides *'Album' framing a vista of the White Garden. (August)*

needed considerable patches and repairs with a mixture of new bricks and the old ones that lay around the site. The gateway through from the tower lawn is marked by a stone plaque of three bishops (looking a little like the Three Wise Men) which the Nicolsons had brought home from Constantinople at the outbreak of the First War; thus the wall is named the Bishopsgate wall.

The garden so enclosed was divided classically on crossing points. The whole rectangle was divided into four with a central square, then each half was again divided, the southern half into another four, and the northern half, immediately outside the cottage's door, was quartered and quartered again into sixteen small beds. The paths in between were laid in old bricks. A wide border of lavender was planted south to north through the whole garden, with an avenue of almond trees. The small beds were filled with roses, some hybrid teas in the smaller beds, and more vigorous species, *R. glauca* (*rubrifolia*), *moyesii* and *rugosa* in the larger beds. In the far corner there was what A. R. Powys called 'a cave' with classical fluted pillars (broken) which was for 'outdoor dining'; this became known as the Erectheum, it was planted with roses and vines and many meals were eaten there.

The Priest's House, like the South Cottage, contributes much to the atmosphere of its garden, and it only figured less prominently in the Nicolsons' affections because it was never part of the Bakers' great house, but always a separate dwelling, probably built for the family chaplain in the seventeenth century.

To the south-west of the Priest's House, between it and the wall of the entrance court, is the area known as Delos, now a rather quiet corner of the garden, which must have been very pretty in Vita's time. It was where they stacked all the large stones unearthed when clearing up the Castle ruins, and these had been laid in rather informal rows and layers alongside the path. Vita wrote that 'the plan was inspired by the island of Delos, where the ruins of the houses have left precisely this kind of little terrace, smothered there by mats of the wild flowers of Greece'.[1] Behind and between the terraces were planted plum and cherry trees, particularly the myrobalan plum of which Vita was very fond. Mats of saxifrages, thymes, aubretias and thrift grew over the stones, with little iris and muscari and other spikelets rising from them. When path and stones were spattered with blossom every spring it must have been enchanting. It was the nearest thing to a rock garden that Sissinghurst ever had, or wanted, but it was also not far from the planted pavement that Vita so desired.

That first idea for white flowers had actually been for the dark corner of the tower lawn where the Lion Pond had failed and been filled in. After the War, the first effort was to revive the garden, and they started with the rose garden, the courtyard and tower lawn, the cottage garden, the lime walk, the nuttery polyanthus and the herb garden; only then did they think about the Priest's House, or the Erectheum garden as it was usually called. They discussed the matter fitfully through early 1949; one problem was that their precious delphiniums, planted beside the path to the front door (on the south side) of the Priest's House had suffered badly from neglect and either needed replacing or scrapping. Vita was for scrapping, and on 8 June she wrote to say she was planning the white and silver planting; a week later, Harold, whilst being drawn by Felix Topolski, came to further decisions about the new planting – 'I think of it as cineraria in masses, rabbit's ears in masses, lad's love, santolina and the whole background being predominantly as grey as the rabbit's ears, then out of this jungle of growth I wish regale to rise . . .'.[2]

Just over two weeks later, he had considered a little more . . . 'I am not happy about the Erectheum garden. I think it is such a lovely shape and we see so much of it that it ought to be turned into a July garden . . . I believe we shall find the grey and white garden very

Opposite *The White Garden seen from the north-east corner in July; the foreground shows the complex pattern of box edged beds each planted with a different species. Beyond the* Rosa mulliganii *bower are the larger beds of silver and grey carpeting plants mixed with white lilies.*

Right *The White Garden in spring; hostas, iris, ferns, white tulips and Solomon's Seal seen from beneath the magnolia by the Bishopsgate. (May)*

Above *Senecio cineraria 'Ramparti' fills one of the beds with a silvery light. (October)*

beautiful . . . I want the garden as a whole to be superb for 1951 for the British Fair or Festival, with heaps of overseas visitors and many will come down by car . . . I should like to concentrate on having at least the Erectheum lovely for July – with regale and silver we shall do that'.[3]

And so it was agreed. Vita got on with her planning and seed collecting, for so many of the plants were already in the garden; she grew the regale lilies from seed and many of the silver plants were lifted from elsewhere and divided. In the following January, 1950, she wrote in the *Observer*, 'I cannot help hoping that the great ghostly barn owl will sweep silently across a pale garden, next summer, in the twilight, the pale garden that I am now planting under the first flakes of snow'.[4]

A potent reason for the fame of this garden, and the reason that it has survived as the most glorious, and most gloriously conserved of Sissinghurst's gardens, is that it was made almost in public. Vita and her garden were now very famous; her *Observer* readers were many, and her greatest fans, and of course they poured into Sissinghurst the next summer in 1950 to see the developments. The garden grew under the watchful, admiring gaze of thousands of pairs of eyes, it was photographed by amateurs and professionals, and written about. It was the veritable celebrity's child, and could hardly make a move without applause, or behave badly without causing disappointment and distress. Vita described the plants in some detail in the *Observer* on 5 July 1955, and three weeks later in *Country Life* Lanning Roper made it clear that this was the most desirable of planting schemes, and that imitation might be the sincerest form of flattery. But the phenomenal child did not seem to have a name. Vita had mentioned her 'all white' flowers ten years earlier, but they were to be planted elsewhere. This garden was the Priest's House or the Erectheum garden; their discussions had wandered around the idea of grey, silver and white. Lanning Roper and *Country Life* specifically called it the grey garden, and the grey and silver garden; Vita herself, having called it her pale garden, also wrote that it was a grey, green, white and silver garden. She wanted it called her White Garth, from the old word for a small enclosure, for undoubtedly its cloistered feeling added much to its charm. I do not know if the exact moment that it acquired its name can be identified; I doubt it. It was rather a pity that Vita did not prevail with her White Garth, which would have been romantic. Certainly, by the time her daughter-in-law Philippa had published *V. Sackville-West's Garden Book* in 1968, it was firmly called the White Garden.

The indecisions about the name were due to difficulties, which it is worth trying to examine across the intervening thirty years since Vita's death. Apart from the slightly anarchic notion that anyone should want to plant a garden to flower in July and August when the beau monde were on holiday, there were ambiguities over the colour white. Purists of course argued that it was no colour at all. Gertrude Jekyll, the voice from Olympus on the subject of colours in the garden, had suggested plants for blue borders, gold borders, grey borders and orange borders. She would not have dreamed of white on its own; for one thing, to her artist's eye, white was the colour of light, to be used in the garden as the Impressionists used it on canvas: to highlight colours and to lighten dark places. Also she would not have flouted the delicate social convention that white, which might be for virgins and brides, was overwhelmingly and inevitably the colour of death.

In response to Miss Jekyll's writings one-colour gardens had a fling; Lady Iveagh planted blue borders and gold borders at Pyrford Court in Surrey (though guests were known to remark that the blue walk made them feel that way), and Norah Lindsay planted double borders of pure blue, blue-greys, blue-purples with touches of white and yellow beside Sir Philip Sassoon's swimming pool at Trent Park in Middlesex. Mrs Lindsay also conspired with Major Johnston in his red borders at Hidcote Manor. And, as

The White Garden seen from the window of the Priest's House, the room in which Vita died on 2 June 1962. (August)

Above *The White Garden in the 1960s when the almond trees formed the central arbour, with narrow arches and hedges and a cluster of flower pots. Rosa 'Nevada' is in bloom beside the hedge, with* Puya alpestris *in the vase.*

Below Tanacetum parthenium *'Rowallane' flowering in October.*

Lanning Roper recalled, there were wonderful grey and pink, grey and orange, and grey and yellow gardens at Brympton d'Evercy in Somerset before the War; this is especially interesting, as these were the schemes that Vita sketched out for her separate raised beds at Long Barn. All these ideas were acceptable to conventional English gardeners. But white, white was the colour of the revolution associated with the renegade Modern Movement; white was the colour to shock, as with Syrie Maugham's all-white rooms, or white concrete modern houses and the all-white flowers that the brothers Paul and Andre Vera put into their witty and irreverent French gardens.

The timing of Sissinghurst's White Garden was a crucial factor in its acceptance, for other flower lovers were ready for it, just ready to rush in where laggard gardeners feared to tread. The pioneering flower arranger, Constance Spry, loved white flowers and grey foliage and had suggested a long list of plants for a white border in her book *Flowers in House and Garden*, which was first published in 1937. After the War it was her encouragement and success that were largely responsible for the rise in interest in flower arranging, in flower clubs and competitions. The White Garden was revealed as one of the first 'flower arranger's gardens', simply because it contained so many wonderful foliage plants and striking white flowers; the emphasis was on the grey and silver foliage especially, as with a good supply of this a very few flowers can be transformed into wonderful arrangements. Undoubtedly, as war-shattered Englishwomen realigned their energies to better things than ration books and utility coupons, many gardeners took up flower arranging and vice versa. Surely amongst the burgeoning flower clubs of southern England one of the highest priorities for the club charabanc-outing was Sissinghurst. It should also be added that the perception of another remarkable lady, the 'silver queen' Mrs Desmond Underwood, fostered the taste that worshipped Sissinghurst's White Garden. She raised her own grey and silver plants at Rampart's Nursery in Colchester and introduced them to gardeners at the Royal Horticultural Shows in the later fifties and the sixties.

Gardens are usually made slowly and quietly, over many years; another unusual aspect of the White Garden is that it was conceived, planted and flowered in breathtaking beauty within about five years. Of course this was largely because its setting, including the yew hedges of the yew walk, the almond trees and lavenders and box, were already grown. But even so, this flowering was fast enough to catch the imagination of a tremendous number of people who were interested both in the garden and in its distinguished makers. Sissinghurst's loyal army of 'shillings', and Vita's faithful *Observer* readers felt involved, almost present at the birth, of this wonder garden. This army still flourishes, and so many people throughout the world, not only keen gardeners, have their memories of this one garden, even if they remember no other. Now, forty years on, it continues to flower exquisitely on the crest of this great wave of nostalgic affection.

The White Garden is a very special place. It is so special that no attempts to analyse its planting will disturb its magic. The whole garden is actually a composition of two different extremes of planting styles – the carpeting beds of grey and silver foliage from which white flowers, particularly the regale lilies that Harold dreamed of, rise, and the complex pattern of box edged boxes into which one single variety is usually planted. The central focus is the arbour of *Rosa mulliganii*. The arbour used to be formed of almond trees, the original avenue tree of the garden, but these have been replaced by a delicate iron tracery, designed by Nigel, which carries the giant canopy of white roses, that have a slight scent of bananas, upon which the flowers arrive without fail – this is a Sissinghurst tradition – on the first of July, and may last through until September.

The first, or southern half, of the garden, with the large beds, is presided over by the demure statue of the Vestal Virgin, cast in lead from the wooden original by Tomas

Rosandic, which stands in the Long Library. The little Virgin was cast in 1935 and she stood in different positions – once at the north end of the almond tree avenue – until she was placed in her present position when these beds were planted. It was Vita's intention that she should be cloaked in the delicate branches of the weeping pear, *Pyrus salicifolia* 'Pendula'. The original tree, a Christmas present in 1939 from her friend – to whom *The Garden* is dedicated – Mrs Katharine Drummond, was also first planted elsewhere, but both weeping pear cloak and frail Virgin came together when the White Garden was made. The original pear was the most tragic victim of the Great Storm of October 1987; fortunately the statue was not damaged and she now encourages the growth of a young replacement. I think it most likely that it was this original tree that introduced *Pyrus salicifolia* to the gardening public, making it so popular that in *Variations on a Garden* (1974), Robin Lane Fox was forced to remark in 1974 that it was 'becoming a status symbol'.[5]

Vita wrote a poem about her little statue, which appeared in her *Collected Poems*:

One of the purposes of the White Garden was to glow in the dusk when the family arrived at the Priest's House for dinner. (August)

127

How slender, simple, shy, divinely chaste,
She wilting stood,
Her suppleness at pause, by leisure graced,
In robes archaic by the chisel woo'd,
That smoothly flowed around her waist
And all her figure traced,
And at her feet in fluid ripples broke;[6]

The White Garden in autumn, with an abundance of white flowerheads, dahlias and Leucanthemella serotina. *This view is from the south-easternmost corner of the garden, and beyond the white blooms the sun catches the canopy of orange heps on* Rosa mulliganii. *The slender little statue of the Virgin emerges from the shade farther to the left. (October)*

The Virgin's whole mood pervades her part of the garden; she gazes out onto the four beds, edged and filled with felty grey stachys and verbascum leaves, lavender and clumps of silver santolina and *Convolvulus cneorum*, creamy gypsophila, white dianthus and bluish hosta leaves. White violas and greeny nicotianas make an appearance; the silvery spires of the verbascums are joined by foxgloves and the pinky veined–flowers of masses

The White Garden, looking eastwards from beneath the canopy of Rosa mulliganii. *The grey vase, which was acquired in the 1930s and is now thought to be Chinese Ming dynasty, is filled with a large* Astelia 'Silver Spear'. *(October)*

of regale lilies. Sometimes there are white hardy geraniums, the towering, silver-sheened *Onopordum acanthium*, white galega (goat's rue), white violas and bluish rue, and a touch of grey-mauve, which inspired Robin Lane Fox – 'Whoever suggested the slate-white hanging tube-flowers of a campanula called *C. burghaltii* deserves my prize for ingenious planting. In full flower, this abundant plant took the edge off the bright whiteness of the main theme . . . this grey-white campanula was well mixed with the glaucous leaves and flowers of hostas . . .'; he also saw the 'garden's glory', the *Cardiocrinum giganteum* which he thought 'summed up the whole strength of the garden's whiteness'.[7]

The northern half of the garden succeeds by contrast with this dazzling show; the dark green of the glossy box edgings for sixteen flower boxes – supplied empty – would delight many a gardener, and foster dreams for filling them in a hundred different ways. I wonder just how many 'fillings' have been tried here – there are lilies, arum lilies amongst glossy green sheaves, sweet-smelling bunches of *Lilium longiflorum*, white roses, the Floribunda 'Iceberg' and 'White Wings', a Hybrid Tea tinged with pink which Vita thought 'divine', white columbines, silvery *Senecio bicolor cineraria* and helichrysums, greeny fennel, cream delphiniums and, as the season fades, white Japanese anemones and michaelmas daisies and dahlias.

Ever since its famous childhood, the White Garden has been praised, photographed and written about. In Vita's lifetime she was both amused and pleased that it should be celebrated in *Vogue* and daily newspapers as well as every gardening magazine. Robin Lane Fox's entertaining *Variations on a Garden*, published in 1974, wide ranging and full of trenchant criticisms where he felt necessary, is a good example of the garden's impact on a younger generation of gardening journalists who were the taste-makers of our time. He was only too well aware of the famous garden, which, he wrote 'has perhaps made more impression on the gardening public than any other planting of the past thirty years. Ever since Vita Sackville-West conceived it ... white gardens have been very much in the night air of English country gardens. I can think of fifteen, at least ...'.[8] He set off to see this phenomenon for the first time, prepared to be disappointed, but he was not – 'Its effect is indeed astonishing ...' may be added to the praises already quoted. That this garden still continues to draw gasps of admiration and delight from gardening taste-makers and gardeners alike is an abiding tribute to the head gardeners Pamela Schwerdt and Sibylle Kreutzberger and the care of the National Trust. This garden seems so perfectly to respond to their skills and ideas and it is the undoubted continuing triumph of Sissinghurst today, the romantic symbol of the spirit of this place which thousands carry off in their hearts to homes all over the world.

The White Garden is more than part of a gardening legend; it has transcended into general folklore, to be celebrated by painters, poets, photographers and essayists. One writer in particular, Richard Church, has caught its magic in words and he is perhaps better qualified to do this than most, as he not only had a deep affinity with Kent, but also as Dorothy Beale's second husband he lived in the Priest's House, from where he would gaze over the garden throughout the seasons. In an essay 'Recognizing Things' from *A Harvest of Mushrooms* (1970), he observes the most private virtues of the spirit of this place –

As I sit here for the first time, in my isolated fragment of the castle, looking out on the main tower across ancient brickwork and an enclosure of hedgebound flower-beds, I can see the snow quilting which covers everything. Yesterday's sunshine melted some of the snow along the boughs of the weeping trees, but it froze again during the night, and now at sunrise the first rays are glancing horizontally through these diamond pendants from every twig, glittering and breaking into prismatic jewellery that almost tinkles as sparrows and tits flutter about seeking hungrily for a morsel of food.

In summer the White Garden is what its name implies, a composition of white flowering plants dominant among them a bed of gigantic delphiniums just to the left of my window. I came to see them by moonlight last summer, and they glowed there like a collection of cathedrals waiting to be disposed around a Christian community yet to be born... That it is in this remote part of Kent [that the] poet Vita Sackville-West and her husband Sir Harold Nicolson enjoyed their privacy, and expressed it by constructing out of some neglected acres of woodland, stream and meadow, what is now one of the most beautiful gardens in Europe. That is no exaggeration, as I can bear witness through my passion for such things, and my travels to indulge it... and now that I have come to live in the midst of it [Sissinghurst] I hope that I shall not grow too accustomed, and take it for granted.

For all who love Sissinghurst, surely the wisdom of Richard Church's understanding is both anthem and watchword.

The west entrance front beneath snow-quilting.

Sissinghurst Castle

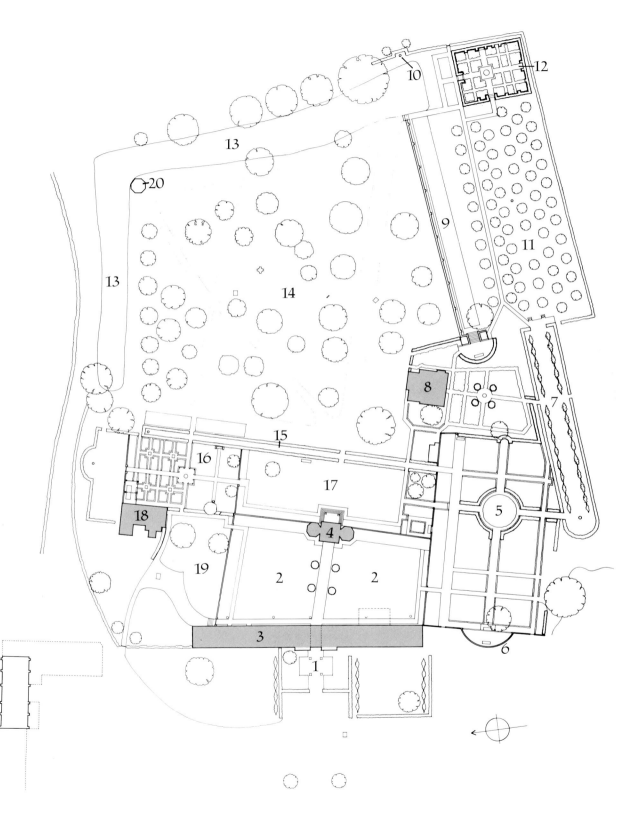

NOTES

1 FOLLOWING IN QUEEN ELIZABETH'S FOOTSTEPS

1 V. Sackville-West, 'Sissinghurst Castle, Kent' in *Country Life*, 4 September 1942, p. 461.

2 For detailed speculation on Sissinghurst's earliest history see Nigel Nicolson, *Sissinghurst Castle: An illustrated history*, National Trust, 1964 pp 3–6.

3 This phrase describes Sir John Baker on the family monument in Cranbrook Church, which was erected in 1736 to commemorate the Baker dynasty who lived at Sissinghurst. The inscription continues: 'And became eminent, as for his abilities in that Profession/So for his Promotion to divers high Posts of Trust and Honour/In the Service of the Crown and State;/Being in Several Parts of his Life,/Recorder of LONDON, Attorney-General, Chancellor of the Exchequer/And Privy Counsellor, to King Henry 8th, King Edward 6th/and Queen Mary. He deceased soon after the Accession of Queen Elizabeth'.

4 This was the theory of A. R. Powys, Secretary of the Society for the Protection of Ancient Buildings, as recorded by V. Sackville-West in her *Country Life* article, *ibid* p. 460.

5 V. Sackville-West, *ibid* p. 458.

6 Quoted by Nigel Nicolson, *ibid* p. 24 from Horace Walpole's letter to Richard Bentley, 9 August 1752.

7 *ibid*.

8 Quoted by Nigel Nicolson, *ibid* p. 26

9 Nigel Nicolson, *ibid*.

10 V. Sackville-West, 'Sissinghurst Castle' in *Country Life*, 28 August 1942, p. 413.

11 Nigel Nicolson, *ibid* p. 39 quoting the inventory of damage held in the Cornwallis archives.

12 Records of the Kent Archaeological Society for the meeting 24–5 July 1873, *Archaeologia Cantiana* vol. IX.

13 V. Sackville-West, 'Sissinghurst Castle' *ibid*.

2 THE NICOLSONS AT HOME

1 See *Vita*, Victoria Glendinning (1983) and *Harold Nicolson* (1980) vol. 1 1886–1929, James Lees-Milne, and suggested further reading list.

2 James Lees-Milne, *Harold Nicolson; A Biography 1930–1968*, vol. 2, 1981, p. 1.

3 Harold Nicolson's exploration of his Irish ancestry, *Helen's Tower* was published in 1937.

4 See my *Vita's Other World*, pp 61–77.

5 V. Sackville-West, 'Sissinghurst Castle', in *Country Life*, 4 September 1942, p. 461.

6 James Lees-Milne, *Harold Nicolson* vol. 2, p. 31.

7 V. Sackville-West, 'The Garden at Sissinghurst Castle, Kent' in *Country Life*, 11 September 1942, p. 506.

8 Harold Nicolson to V. Sackville-West, letter 8 June 1937 quoted on page 131 *Vita's Other World* (original in Lilly Library, Bloomington, Indiana, USA).

9 Harold Nicolson, diary entry on his 50th birthday in 1936, quoted on pp 179–81 *Vita's Other World* and from his 80th birthday card, 21 November 1966 in Sissinghurst Papers.

10 Leter to the author, 5 June 1989.

11 Quoted by V. Glendinning in *Vita*, p. 406.

3 SISSINGHURST AND THE NATIONAL TRUST

1 Vita's legacy explained to the author by Nigel Nicolson in two letters 31 January 1985 and 17 January 1990.

2 Luisa Vertova Nicolson, letter to the author 29 August 1989.

3 Luisa Vertova Nicolson, *ibid*.

4 Benedict Nicolson CBE CVO, editor of the *Burlington Magazine*, died suddenly in London in 1978, aged 63.

5 See John Cornforth, *The Inspiration of the Past*, Viking 1985 p. 134.

6 Quoted in *Vita* p. 380.

7 Castle Drogo, Drewsteignton, Devon was built between 1910–30 to fulfil Julius Drewe's precise romantic notion of a 13th century castle.

8 See my essay on Frances Wolseley in *Eminent Gardeners: Some People of Influence and their Gardens 1880–1980*, Viking, London 1990, and Dawn Macleod *Down-to-Earth Women*, Blackwood, Edinburgh 1982, pp 144–8 on Beatrix Havergal and Waterperry.

9 Anne Scott-James, *Sissinghurst: The Making of a Garden*, p. 126.

10 The detailed history of the National Trust's development of the Chief Gardens Adviser's role will be found in John Gaze, *Figures in a Landscape: A History of the National Trust*, Barrie & Jenkins 1988.

4 THE VIEW FROM THE TOWER

1 *Absence*, V. Sackville-West, Collected Poems, Hogarth Press, London 1933 p. 254

2 *Family History*, V. Sackville-West, Hogarth Press, London 1932 p. 221.

3 Quoted by Anne Scott-James *ibid* p. 90.

5 THE ROSE GARDEN

1 Harold Nicolson, *Diary*, 20 March 1932, quoted in full in *Vita's Other World*, p. 119.

2 V. Sackville-West, 'The Garden at Sissinghurst Castle, Kent' *ibid*, p. 508.

3 *ibid* pp 508–9.

4 David Austin, *A Handbook of Roses*, 16th ed. 1988, p. 22, David Austin Roses, Bowling Green Lane, Albrighton, Wolverhampton.

5 *V. Sackville-West's Garden Book* ed. Philippa Nicolson, 1968 p. 144.

6 *Vita's Other World*, p. 186 quoting V. Sackville-West, *Observer*, 25 August 1957 and *Even More For Your Garden*, p. 132.

7 V. Sackville-West, *The Garden*, Michael Joseph 3rd imp 1947, p. 86.

8 Vita listed rose suppliers in the back of *More for Your Garden*, 1955 ed.

9 Constance Spry, *Flowers for House and Garden*, with a long list of plants for a 'white' garden was published by Dent 1937.

10 V. Sackville-West, *In Your Garden*, p. 187

6 THE LIME WALK AND THE NUTTERY

1 Harold Nicolson (quoted by James Lees-Milne, vol 2 *ibid*, p. 226).

2 Harold Nicolson to V. Sackville-West, 28 April 1936, leter quoted in *Vita's Other World*, p. 181 and original in Lilly Library, Indiana *ibid*.

3 Harold Nicolson *Diary* on his 50th birthday, 1936 see note 9 Chapter 2 for full references.

4 V. Sackville-West to Harold Nicolson, letter March 1952 n.d. quoted in full *Vita's Other World*, p. 182.

7 THE COTTAGE GARDEN, SISSINGHURST CRESCENT AND THE MOAT WALK

1 V. Sackville-West's t ribute to William Robinson in 'Gardens and Gardeners' in *Country Notes*, her *New Statesman* articles, Michael Joseph, 1939.

2 William Robinson, *The English Flower Garden*, John Murray 3rd ed., 1893.

3 Anne Scott-James, *The Cottage Garden*, Allen Lane 1981, p. 118.

4 Margery Fish, *Cottage Garden Flowers*, Collingridge, London and Transatlantic Arts, Florida 1961 p. 112.

5 V. Sackville-West, *In Your Garden 1951*, p. 89.

6 Luisa Vertova Nicolson, letter to the author 29 August 1989.

7 V. Sackville-West, *In Your Garden*, p. 90.

8 THE ORCHARD, THE HERB GARDEN AND THE LAKE

1 Graham Stuart Thomas, *The Old Shrub Roses*, Phoenix House 4th ed., 1963 p. 204. Vita wrote a short foreword to this book.

2 Leter, Harold Nicolson to V. Sackville-West, 18 October 1937.

3 Letter, V. Sackville-West to Harold Nicolson 8 October 1952.

4 Geoffrey Grigson, *The Englishman's Flora*, Phoenix House/Dent, facsimile ed. 1987, p. 226.

5 V. Sackville-West, The Garden, *ibid* p. 89.

9 THE WHITE GARDEN

1 These origins of Delos are described by Vita in 'The Garden at Sissinghurst Castle' *Country Life, ibid* p. 508.

2 Letter, Harold Nicolson to V. Sackville-West 15 June 1949.

3 Letter, Harold Nicolson to V. Sackville-West 4 July 1949.

4 V. Sackville-West *In Your Garden*, p. 21.

5 Robin Lane Fox, *Variations on a Garden*, Readers 'Union' Newton Abbot, 1974, p. 95.

6 V. Sackville-West, 'On the Statue of a Vestal Virgin by Toma Rosandic' in *Collected Poems*, p. 255.

7 Robin Lane Fox *ibid*, p. 95.

8 Robin Lane Fox *ibid*, p. 92.

FURTHER READING

Aslet, Clive *The Last Country Houses*, Yale, 1982.

Brown, Jane *The English Garden in our Time*, Antique Collectors' Club, 1986.

Brown, Jane *Vita's Other World: a gardening biography of V. Sackville-West*, Viking, 1985.

Church, Richard *A Harvest of Mushrooms and other Sporadic Essays*, Heinemann, 1970.

Cornforth, John *The Inspiration of the Past*, Viking, 1985.

Fox, Robin Lane *V. Sackville-West's Garden Book* (ed. Illustrated version) Michael Joseph 1986.

Fox, Robin Lane *Variations on a Garden* R & L (Lane Fox), 1974 re-issue 1989.

Gaze, John *Figures in a Landscape: A History of the National Trust*, Barrie and Jenkins, 1988.

Glendinning, Victoria *Vita: The Life of Vita Sackville-West* Weidenfeld and Nicolson 1983.

Greeves, Lydia and Trinick, Michael *The National Trust Guide*, National Trust, 1989.

Hobhouse, Penelope *The National Trust: A Book of Gardening* Pavilion/M. Joseph, 1986.

Lees-Milne, James *Harold Nicolson: A Biography*, 2 vols, Chatto & Windus, 1980.

Nicolson, Harold *The Desire to Please*, Constable 1943 and subs eds.

Nicolson, Harold *Helen's Tower*, Constable, 1937.

Nicolson, Nigel ed. *Harold Nicolson's Letters and Diaries*, 3 vols, Collins 1966, 1967 and 1968.

Nicolson, Nigel *Kent* Weidenfeld and Nicolson, 1988

Nicolson, Nigel *Portrait of a Marriage*, Weidenfeld and Nicolson, 1973 and illustrated edition 1990.

Nicolson, Nigel *Sissinghurst Castle: An Illustrated History*, The National Trust, 1964 and subs eds.

Olson, Stanley *Harold Nicolson, Diaries and Letters 1930-64* edited and condensed, Penguin Books, Lives & Letters, 1984.

Ottewill, David *The Edwardian Garden*, Yale, 1989.

Sackville-West, V. *The Garden*, Michael Joseph, 1946 and in one edition with *The Land* ed. by Nigel Nicolson, 1989.

Sackville-West, V. *Sissinghurst*, Hogarth Press, 1931.

Sackville-West, V. *Passenger to Teheran*, Hogarth Press, 1926.

Sackville-West, V. *Twelve Days*, Hogarth Press, 1928.

Sackville-West, V. *In Your Garden, In Your Garden Again* and *More for Your Garden*, Michael Joseph, 1951, 1953, 1955 (original vols of *Observer* pieces edited into *V. Sackville-West's Garden Book* by Philippa Nicolson, published 1968. See Robin Lane Fox above.)

Scott-James, Anne *Sissinghurst: The Making of a Garden*, Michael Joseph, 1974.

Scott-James, Anne *The Cottage Garden*, Allen Lane, 1981.

Stevens, Michael *V. Sackville-West: A Critical Biography*, Michael Joseph, 1973.

Thomas, Graham Stuart *The National Trust Book of Gardens*, Weidenfeld and Nicolson, 1979.

INDEX